Acknowledgements

This book is dedicated to my family and close friends without them I would not be alive today.

One thing I have learned is that friends come and go like the change of the tide. Some push you forward, some hold you back, but it all contributes to your personal development.

This book was written during a confusing time in my life where I had to make some very hard judgements about people. Some parts sound bitter or negative because that is a true representation of how I felt at the time. In no way is it about judgement or condemnation — it's about change and reflection. I am a totally different person to the one I was when I began this journey. However I cherish the drama I went through to allow me to reach where I am now.

Key friends I would personally like to thank;

Karen

Mum, Dad, Mark & Peter

Harry Da Silva & Shane Hennah

Chris Hill & Steve Donohue

Lee Kamara, Steve Fowell & Lee Carroll

Kaj Taylor & Steve Dimmock

Richard Atkinson, Neil Cole & Chris Rowe

Falmouth Spiritual Church

Paul Dean & Liam Davies

I am grateful for having such great people behind me.

To Liam Crouse; thank you for your hard effort. Without your tireless will this book would never have been released.

To my Girlfriend Karen; thanks for restoring my faith in love. You are my soul mate.

But the greatest debt of gratitude goes to my beloved family who kept me warm and sheltered when I was homeless and destitute;

My mum, who never complained once and showed me love and compassion through my darkest times.

My father, who was a rock of healing and support and whose advice through my troubles was sound and beneficial. Thank you for the work and skills you have given to me.

My two brothers, whose support and help I am eternally thankful for.

To my boys... I hope you understand this book as you get older. You have made me very proud and you taught me by being born that life is just so precious you can never take from the world without putting back in. Learn from me as I have learned from you.

My grandfather, Tom, who was an inspiration and a guiding light to so many. Bless you and Grandma.

Finally my Nan, who taught me to convey unconditional love by helping others and let go of judgement. You truly were a remarkable person.

I learned so much from these individuals. They showed me the path to human kindness and to always help a friend in need without question. God bless you and thank you for helping me to achieve my goals.

I lost a lot of material things during the creation of this book and now live with my beautiful girlfriend in Cornwall. I have met a lot of very unfortunate people during my journey who have not had the luxury of friends and family along the way. It's easy to forget that they are what bind us together.

I am truly thankful for my life and having the opportunity to tell my story.

Never lose sight of what's important.

"War is Madness, to survive Madness one must become Madness, but must live with Sadness"

Cpl Martin Webster

Voices of War, 2006

CORPORAL MARTIN WEBSTER

Born in Truro, Cornwall in 1976, Martin Webster is the eldest son of a builder and a care worker. He grew up in Falmouth, Cornwall where he attended school and went on to complete a diploma at Falmouth College of Art.

Martin worked as a trainee manager at a local supermarket but this did not satisfy his hunger for life experience. He saw the Army as an excellent opportunity to escape from his home town. After loving every minute of basic training he realised that it would provide the physical and mental challenge he needed to achieve his goals in life.

His first operational tour of Northern Ireland came in 1996, an intense introduction to duty for a 19-year-old lad who had progressed from a supermarket checkout to the bloody riots and IRA terrorists of South Armagh.

He returned from duty in 1997 and, after boxing for his battalion, found himself going down the wrong path.

However the Army had faith in his ability as a soldier and after disciplinary measures he was retained within his career.

Martin went on to achieve the rank of Corporal. After further tours, including to Sierra Leone in 2001, he started writing music and painting art together with Fellow soldiers Lee Kamara and Lee Carroll.

Martin was stationed in Iraq between October 2003 and March 2004. In February 2006 a short video clip which showed British soldiers beating Iraqi civilians was aired on the news and sent shock waves through Britain and the rest of the world.

The rest, as they say, is history.

1. Cannon Fodder

When does a man become an animal? At what point does a soldier turn his back on the rules and call upon his instincts to survive the horror in front of his eyes?

I was the voice behind the camera that the world heard in February 2006, providing commentary as nine British soldiers dished out a beating to Iraqi youths behind a palace in Amarah.

You heard the story as spun by the media, and the one leaked from the MOD press office — you may have even had the story from the Iraqi boys who were arrested. But you never heard our side, the side that when told is not glorifying war, nor trying to show ourselves as heroes or men of honor.

We were just men thrown into an extreme situation. One that has been kept very quiet since the incident faded from public view. I have a duty to explain what happened and to show the reality of war...

I grew up in a small town called Falmouth, and after leaving school I worked at a Co-op stacking shelves and doing warehouse work. But I wasn't fulfilled and needed to escape — I yearned for something that would whisk me away on an adventure.

First I tried out for the Navy. After failing the entrance test miserably (which I now believe was due to Dyslexia or learning difficulties) I was told by the recruitment officer that I should try downstairs where the Army might have a job for me.

As I walked past recruitment signs on the way out, a stocky man with a broken nose and a rack of medals shouted to me, "Fancy joining us in Cyprus for some sun, sea and adventure, mate?"

I gazed at the poster advertising a posting in Cyprus for two years — it looked just the ticket.

"How long before I can get in?"

"Don't you worry about that, son. I can get you in within 6 weeks."

"Sign me up!"

How fast can you run? How many pull ups can you do? Are you gay? Have you ever done drugs? How do you feel about killing someone? These were some of the questions that I can remember having to answer.

"I'm Sgt Williams of 2LI" he said, "Now — watch this fucking video."

I sat there watching this film production glorifying life in the forces. To be honest I didn't have a clue what I was going for, but as long as I got to shoot people and throw grenades that was all I was really interested in.

After a touch screen test I was given my results by the Sergeant.

"Right, son... you have scored really well and all of your results point to the best job in the Army; the Infantry.

"This is what you can go for; Sniper, Rifleman, or how about Anti-tank Missileman? Or even a Mortar Fire Controller?"

"I like the sound of that one Sergeant." I said.

"Or like me," he grinned, "a Mortarman firing bombs at the enemy. How does that sound?"

If only I had known that my score was equivalent to that of a chimpanzee, hence why he was reading me a list of jobs within one department of the whole British Army.

But he'd appealed to my nature with the promise of action and travel.

***

"Granddad, I'm in!" I said enthusiastically as I jumped in the car. The poor man had waited for 6 hours in the car park for me.

"You're in what?" he said in his Liverpool Accent.

"The Light Infantry"

"Oh, cannon fodder. That's nice, your mum will be pleased!" he said, rolling his eyes. "No, honestly... well done son. It will be the making of you."

Cheers Granddad.

***

His sarcastic comment hadn't been far wrong. Mum was worried they'd send me to Northern Ireland but I'd managed to convince her I was on my way to Cyprus for two years.

"You won't last two days" my dad had mumbled with a smirk.

But his prediction wasn't so accurate — within a matter of months I was training and loving every second of it. I had finally found my role in life.

I met a Northern lad through training called Barry Sherriff. In March 1996 we were on our last week, waiting to find out where our first postings would be. The Platoon Sergeant came around to brief us up.

"Listen up, dickheads," he barked, "two choices; Bosnia or Northern Ireland, as the paddies have just denounced the ceasefire."

I was shocked at the change of plans, but also excited... this is what we had joined up for.

"What happened to Cyprus?" said Sherriff

I wasn't thinking about that. I was in the British Army and that's all that mattered. I couldn't wait to start my job as an Infantry Soldier. I was so proud.

Six years later in 2002, after tours of Northern Ireland, Sierra Leone and countless other adventures around the globe, I found myself at Paderborn in Germany awaiting orders for war.

Following September 11th 2001 things in the world were changing rapidly.

Little did I know how much it would affect me personally.

2. Operation Fresco

It was 2002 and all the soldiers were lining up to get our anthrax inoculations. There was some paperwork to complete; a form which said words to the effect of "In the event of side effects after the six needle course, the Ministry of Defence holds no responsibility". There was also a DVD issued to explain these possible side effects. I heard it was rubbish.

Once the forms were completed there was excitement in the air; we were now an armoured battalion and had completed our conversion with top marks. We were able to celebrate at the Christmas dinner, where all the officers and senior ranks serve the junior ranks. A hush fell over the room as the Commanding Officer got up to deliver his annual speech.

"It's looking good gents... in fact, it's never looked this good. We are quite possibly going to get our greatest challenge so far in going to war, but the hard work has paid off. We have impressed the right people by converting to the armored role so quickly and I am so proud to take such an excellent fighting force to war. Thank you and your families for your efforts."

The applause nearly took the roof off. We were going to war — it was the most exciting feeling I had felt in my seven year career. The CO had been involved in the first Gulf War and countless other military campaigns with the Special Forces. Not only a pure legend, but also a really likable and respected character was leading our battalion into battle.

***

Christmas leave had ended. I'd just finished with my ex-girlfriend so with the new year came an opportunity for a fresh start.

Soldiers and friends, some of whom I hadn't seen for years, regrouped at the guardroom in Paderborn nervously waiting to find out what was happening.

"Fucking ragheads ruined my leave!" said Chris Ainsworth, "We'd better go now after all this palaver" He hadn't long had his first child. War wasn't top of the agenda for him and a lot of the other married men.

But me and my mate Liam, a fellow soldier from Falmouth, were okay; the only relationships we had were with our right hands (or anything we could pull down at Savoy's night club on a Saturday night). We had recently bought a property each in Spain and were planning on going out after the war to run our own bar down in the Costa. But we were now focused on the mission ahead; it had been a long 11 years since the first Gulf War.

We were in for a surprise. At Friday fitness, the CO took to the parade square and announced;

"We're not going to war anymore — they're sending 7 Armoured Brigade instead."

I felt sick. It was the worst let-down ever.

"We are sending two companies to help them; A Company and D Company. I will be leaving soon."

His cool professional manner made him appear blunt but we later found out that he was absolutely gutted and had wanted to turn down promotion so that he could take the boys he trained to war.

'A/D Coy?'

I thought, 'Hmm, there is still a chance I can get on this safari...'

I started trying to come up with ways I could join in. I was in Fire Support Company but also had the right qualifications for Rifle Company. Where there's a will, there's a way — but time was running out.

I caught up with the old CO in the Cpl's mess and asked him what had gone wrong. He told me it would have been 20 Armored Brigade but apparently Turkey had been opposed to us using their country's rail line as access to Iraq's back door.

Luckily for us his replacement, Terry Hilling, was pretty good also.

I went to my OC to see if he could help me.

"Sir, can I have a word please?" I asked. He knew what I was going to ask before I even had a chance to say it.

"No CPL Webster, no one has dropped out yet and no, we have no available spaces, but the minute we do we will consult you first. Now go away."

The next day CSM McCulloch popped his head round the office door.

"Right CPL Webster — stop hassling all company commanders, you are not going and that's final."

***

As if not going to war wasn't bad enough we got hit with a rumour that we were to take part in Operation Fresco

 — the fire strikes. I thought it was a wind-up. The British Army is preparing for war and we had to put fires out because the fire service was trying to hold the government to ransom for more wages.

A and D company were all walking around in their desert kit and they had the new 7th Armoured Brigade 'Desert Rats' flashes on their sleeves. They looked cool as fuck — I had never felt so jealous in all my life.

We all mounted the bus in Paderborn, Germany. The lads who were going waved at us with big fat grins on their faces as we drove towards England with our heads in our hands.

Thoughts ran through my brain of A and D Coy sharpening bayonets and getting psyched up for conflict, while we were demoted to fire duties. It had been made clear to me that there wasn't a chance of getting out to Iraq as long as I had a hole in my ass.

The training, based in the Midlands, was a piece of piss. When they brought out the green goddess fire engines they looked like they belonged in a museum; they were made of wood and therefore not particularly suitable for being close to naked flames. On top of that our combats, once washed many times, were flammable, effectively making us human torches waiting to be lit. Ironic, wasn't it?

The firemen training us were complete health-and-safety freaks. The officer had to explain everything in his brief.

"Right — when at a fire don't try to be brave. If a fire has been going for half an hour and you see someone at the window, don't go running into the house trying to save them. Anything that's been in there more than thirty minutes is considered matter and you're not to risk your life. Your kit and equipment is not designed to fight fire."

"So why don't you just give us your equipment?" someone asked.

"Because you're not trained" was the reply.

'Listen mate'

, I was thinking, 'we're the British Army — show us what to do and we will just get the job done, we don't need to go on strike.'

Clearly the Fire Brigade wanted us to fail.

We began the three day training package, learning about a 1930 generator to pump water from rivers, how to make an A-frame and putting out burning cars. For the first time we started smiling and accepting that we weren't going to war.

"Bine me crow," said big Andy Buller, jabbing me in the arm until I gave him a fag. Andy was our boss and really wanted to go to war, even though he had a year left from 24.

"This will be all right mate. We'll just put 100% into it. Just wasn't meant to be, and that's that." He was good at putting things into context.

Under Andy was Jono who was the platoon sergeant. We didn't have an officer in charge so the platoon worked really well. That's not a dig at officers — it's just that, from my experience, a lot of them are arrogant and can cause friction amongst platoons.

We had finished the training and were getting a debrief from the fire officer. He said "Not a bad effort, despite small errors, such as not wearing special gloves to check over the hose and handle the nozzles and segments."

"So what are we supposed to do if we haven't got any?" I asked.

"Well then, you can't do it."

See, that was the difference between the British Army and the fire brigade at the time; we would do anything to achieve our mission.

3. Misplaced Rage

A letter from the front line...

'Fucking hot... lots of Saddam's Army putting up a poor fight... shot 2 already; me and Natty kicked in the door of this building and shot the enemy right up! Killing killing killing, I love it here! Wish you were here Webby...

Sgt Chalky White'

Webby was my nickname and the soldiers in my regiment knew I would have sold a kidney to go out to Iraq. At the time I liked the idea of going to war, engaging in battle and killing the enemy.

Reading the letter from Chalky made me feel sick with envy. How could I ever work with these guys again? We were no longer in the same league.

That letter reminded me that my best friend Liam was out there and I started to wonder how he was doing. 'He'd better not get fucking killed!'

I thought to myself, 'We've got a business in Spain to start after this shit's over.'

So I sent him a letter to cheer him up. It went like this:

'Hope you're okay Liam, but I wish I was out there as well.

I've sent you some light snacks to keep you going through the day. I hear the Fusiliers have got no desert clothing and the food is the same menu. No change there with the Support from Government! Really though mate, hope you come back safe.

Yours so jealously,

Webby'

I filled the envelope with my toe nails and pubic hair because I knew it would make him laugh.

Saddam had Weapons of Mass Destruction and could target the UK in 45 minutes. This is what our Prime Minister had told us. I turned on the TV in March 2003 and watched the historic moments as they began to topple Saddam Hussein from power. I prayed for a swift victory so that we could all get back to normal as quickly as possible.

I also read in the papers about Colonel Tim Collins and his magnificent speech in the desert. Soldiers need to hear this kind of dialect before battle; it spurs them on to do great things as the British Army is truly a force to be reckoned with when they believe in a just cause.

***

I had managed to get myself onto a UK Special Forces course, but still needed something to take my mind off the war effort. While home in Cornwall doing some training I met with a friend in the Royal Marines who was on Special Forces selection in a year's time. 'The Moose' we called him, and he was incredibly fit and one hard bastard.

We went out in Falmouth for a drink. Everybody we saw who knew us would say 'What are you doing here? Why aren't you out fighting the war?' I was gutted but it helped to share the let down with someone else.

Let me explain something about my hometown; Falmouth is one of the most beautiful places in Cornwall, but some of the local lads are fucking crazy and not afraid to fight anyone. It has always been like that, but boy do I love that town.

We went to the local 'O.K. Corral' — a place called Club International where all the mad men hang out. We carried on drinking and the idea of missing out on war really began to eat at me.

"We have missed the party, the whole fucking war! All that training and there probably won't be another one now for ten years!" I said. Moose agreed.

Suddenly all hell broke loose as two blokes at the bar started fighting. We were stood there watching them knock fuck out of each other when The Moose ducked a punch that ended up landing on me! I wasn't about to take that, so me and Moose decided to treat ourselves for missing the war.

We jumped in and quickly finished what they had started. I smacked one of the blokes fighting and knocked him to the floor. As I walked towards the night club exit I got the impression that the bouncers were pleased me and Moose had ended the scrap.

As I walked down the street, I could hear someone screaming at me — the bloke I had just decked had picked himself up and followed me outside. As I turned around he flew in with a punch that missed. Grabbing him by his hair, I punched his cheek bone till it cracked before concentrating jabs to his wind pipe to finish him off.

We had blood all over our shirts. He got back up and tried again.

"Listen mate — go home or I will kill you..." I warned, but he lunged at me again and hit me very hard in the face. I knew this could go on all night as he wasn't just some mug — he could handle himself.

This time I grabbed his face and screwed my thumb into his eye socket. He screamed in pain. I stepped back and we both knew this was pointless.

The British Army had spent years training me to kill. That's what I knew and that's what I was paid to do. To control that is another thing — something I struggled with.

This is the brutality of a frontline soldier and some people will find it very hard to understand, but this was our way — we used anger and hatred to dominate any enemy.

What I did that night I know was wrong — to take my hunger for combat out on a civilian was not a just cause. We are supposed to defend the nation.

I was wrong and I'm sorry to that lad.

I got back from UK Special Forces selection early because of a back injury. I wasn't cut out for that role — I was too much of a gobshite and had a lot to learn.

All the lads were back from Iraq and we had a ban in the mess; no talking about the war because the jealousy would cause fights. Of course no one paid any attention to that rule... a few of the guys who probably did sod-all were at the bar chanting "war dodgers". It wasn't nice. But then we were thrown a lifeline — the news spread that we would be going back out to Iraq in October 2003.

We were so excited. The new OC Major James Pearce had taken over with my old platoon sergeant, Craig McCulloch, as CSM, so we had some good leaders in charge. We were going to get our war after all...

4. Picking Up Brass

"This is your new company commander." said CSM McCulloch.

In walked Major James Pearce — a slim man with red hair and a unique voice. I was unsure about him based on how he looked until my good friend H Hanley reassured me;

"That bloke is the best commander I have ever worked with and he will be awesome in Iraq." Those words were good enough for me as Hanley was one of the corporals I worked with in Sierra Leone and a very good leader himself.

"We are going to Masan Province, the marsh land tribes; these people are the fiercest fighters in Iraq and Saddam never controlled this area." James Pearce said with a PowerPoint presentation behind him. "What chance have we

got then?" I said to Browny, a guy who was in my team for Iraq. We had a good line up for our tour. Our company's men were the finest quality soldiers I had served with throughout the Northern Ireland tours and Sierra Leone. Working together in extreme circumstances helps you to form a bond. Major Pearce knew this and his leadership was the icing on the cake that we needed.

We had a tight schedule to deploy to Iraq but no one questioned it — we just wanted to get out there so were careful not to do anything to jeopardise that. A strict fitness regime was put in place, including four runs a week carrying specialised weapons such as sniper rifles, mortar barrels and

Milan post anti-tank missile systems. Fire Support Company did a different role from the others — we were the backup.

We were sent on a two week package which involved training activities and insights into what we might face out in Iraq. We all felt very confident about our mission brief from Major Pearce but the training seemed to be non-existent. In fact we only had two weeks in contrast to six to eight months before deployment to Northern Ireland. The Multiple was also briefed by ISAF who had very limited knowledge as the situation in Iraq was constantly changing. On top of this, we still had no Rules of Engagement.

Liam, the friend I had sent the letter to, had already been out to Iraq during the invasion and had told us some harrowing reports about the hostility they faced.

"We just got swamped by them in the village and they would hurl stones the size of apples at us, every time.

"The ungrateful mob... the place stank and so did their treatment of us."

At the time I didn't really care. I just wanted to get out there.

We were given a riot training package beforehand — a couple of days in a mock-up village where we were formed up into our section and multiples for the tour.

It was all very thrown together but I wasn't complaining.

In my team was Browny, Mac and Calvert — good quality men; very professional. Browny had joined up at the same time as me and we had a good friendship. He was fun to be around and you need a morale booster in the squad.

Our job was to do patrols around the pretend village. The Royal Engineers were playing the parts of both Iraqi civilians and the enemy. They were taking it very seriously and had just taken out one of my men.

Cpl Bobby Moore came into our bunker, screaming, "Those engineers are being real pricks!"

I chuckled to myself before turning to my team;

"No one is going to get the better of us, training exercise or not — we fight like they are the real enemy"

"Okay Webby" they agreed. They may have been giving us a right hammering in the village but would be no match for Fire Support Company's experience of Northern Ireland's Drumcree riots where we faced a 3,000+ UVF stronghold. We were battle-hardened warriors and 100 Royal Engineers weren't about to change that.

As we retreated to the confines of our pretend base CSM McCulloch shouted out:

"It's not over lads — I think they're going to hit us with the suicide bomber scenario."

My team was chosen to act as a barrier to keep the crowd back.

"If they penetrate the compound wall we will use the Land Rovers to block the gap and send out a human barrier, rifles cocked and ready" I said. "If they rush us, shoot a member of the crowd and see if they back off."

There was a large 'boom' as a simulation grenade went off. It was the training staff opening the compound gate who said;

"Right, a suicide bomber has blown open your gates... what are you going to?"

We were already in position as the rioters closed in fast.

"Stand back, stand back or we will shoot!" we shouted.

The crowd loomed in and we stood in a very aggressive stance, peering over our rifle sights at the rioters trying to flank and capture one of us. They were the real deal in my eyes.

"Come on, shoot us then!" screamed a rioter as he grabbed the end of my rifle and tried to drag me into the crowd. Without hesitating I pulled the trigger. The sound of my weapon firing caused the crowd to rush back suddenly as the man dropped to the floor, clutching his throat in agony.

A member of the safety team grabbed hold of me and screamed in my ear "It's just pretend you fucking idiot!" but I ignored him and told my men to stand their ground. Major Pearce ordered us to slowly withdraw into the building and I did so, still in an aggressive stance, treating it as real until the last moment. These were my friends; no one was going to hurt them. If you're on my side, I will put my life on the line to protect you.

"Come here you stupid boy!" The safety staff grabbed me again, trying to lead me off to the side.

"Fuck off!" I snarled back at him. He knew me well, as he had trained me at Depot, and allowed me to carry on.

I turned to Major Pearce and the CSM and said, all flustered;

"My section are all present and correct."

"I want him charged ASAP" said the safety officer. Major Pearce paid no attention and moved us into a corner of the building.

"Outstanding! What a force to be going to Iraq with. All of you, well done." said the Major.

"Sorry, Sir, for losing it and shooting that man." I said.

"Webby shut up, you did well" he replied with a smile. "Now fuck off!"

None of the safety team seemed to share this view and the after brief was a different story. One said; "What is the safety distance with a blank firing attachment on your rifle, Webster?"

I replied "50 meters, Sir."

"Good, well done. That was an officer you shot point blank in the face, he is now in hospital having brass shrapnel picked out of his neck and is in much pain."

"He should not have tried to take my weapon Sir. I issued two challenges for him to back off. Under the Rules of Engagement that's what it states in the yellow card." I said.

"Don't be cocky, you might be charged if the officer wants to pursue this matter."

Unhappily I muttered under my breath "Yes, whatever" as the lads around all sniggered.

The job we were going to Iraq to do was essentially clearing up after the other soldiers who did the fighting. In the military the job was known as 'picking up brass'. That officer I shot was now picking brass out of his face.

Little did we know a storm was brewing that would mean it would turn out very differently.

5. "Have A Nice Flight"

Our flight out was with Argentina Airways. Being as the seats on the plane were filled with soldiers' asses the cabin absolutely stank after ten minutes. I doubt it was very nice for the air hostesses, who were really sexy and smelled lovely. I was living in Spain at the time so tried my Spanish out on some of them and managed to get an email address. I was on a high.

A member of the crew announced over the tannoy system, "Thank you for flying with Argentina Airways ladies and gentlemen, you will shortly be arriving in Basra airport. The local time is 1300 and the outside temperature is 38 degrees. Have a safe tour and we wish you all good luck."

Then Nat Marks added, at the top of his voice "Rob Wills, I hope you get your legs blown off!" Good old soldier humour.

The plane doors opened and as I stepped out I was hit by the intense heat followed closely by the toxic smell of burning oil. I wasn't thinking about how we were about to introduce democracy to the Iraqi people and liberate their country; all that was going through my mind as I walked down the steps was, 'how do I survive this?'

Personal survival: that comes first, always. This view may not be shared by deluded White Hall pen-pushers and politicians sat around back home scratching their heads but it is the way life is for a soldier; you just need to survive the six month tour.

***

Later that night Liam and I gazed into the distance at the burning oil refineries.

"Do you think that's why we're really here?" Liam asked me.

"Suppose so. Well, we all drive cars." We all knew in the back of our minds that we weren't there solely to help this country.

Either way, I didn't give a shit about Foreign policy or democracy at the time. I just cared about my friends.

6. Rear Echelon MF

When we arrived we were taken to the hangar and shown a video about land mines and UXO. We were given flat jackets and a packed lunch and had to sit on a sweaty coach while some Arab on the radio wailed like he was in pain.

We were learning all the time. I had done two tours of Jordan in '97 and '98 so I understood the Arab culture more than the younger guys.

"Browny, we can't be far from Shaiba logistics base can we?" I said. "We're on coaches and we've got no ammo for our rifles"

"Hope not, Webby mate." Browny replied.

And off we went. For some reason, everyone seemed to think that closing the curtains would turn us invisible — as if the Iraqis wouldn't suspect that the convoy of seven large coaches, with Land Rovers at the front and back for protection, was in fact the British Army.

We were being led by the biggest fuckwits the Army had — the Royal Military Police, or RMP. They had what we call 'chef's webbing' — their equipment was hanging off them and made them look shit. And if they looked like shit, it probably meant they were shit.

There were two per vehicle armed with SA80 rifles to protect the relieving battle group. That worked out at about 600 bullets ready to go down to suppress the enemy and protect 500+ unarmed men. Theoretically, the local militia could have wiped us out before we even arrived — a whole battle group storming conspicuously through the desert. Whoever organised the logistics for this cluster fuck should have lost their rank. It was criminal negligence.

How the Iraqis never took us out is beyond me. Maybe they pitied us and thought they'd give us a chance.

***

Four hours later we arrived at Shaiba logistical base or, as it was known at the time, 'Shibiza' on account of all the REMFs (Rear Echelon Mother Fuckers) based there. RAF parties, shagging... yep, these REMFS had it real tough.

Looking back now our lack of respect for the other team efforts within the military machine would often hamper our ability to get on with other units. But this had always been the same. Infantry always got the shitty end of the stick.

We would be here in comfort for one week before heading north to Amarah.

7. Rat's Cock

A week before we deployed the Territorial Army had arrived with no training whatsoever. It was disgusting but the government seemed to be breaking all the rules to make this war work.

On our first day in Iraq, Fingers came out and introduced one of the TA lads from his team.

"How long have you been in mate?" I asked.

"Two weeks"

"Two weeks?" I said, shocked, "What's your job back home?"

The lad told me he was a chemist who had joined the TA just six weeks ago. He was sent a letter after a fortnight and sent to Iraq. He said he had never even seen an SA80 until yesterday.

"No way! That's illegal, surely?" said Liam.

This was a situation I had never heard of. Our government sending civilians with no training into fully fledged war. This was a story perhaps not unfamiliar in the First World War... but it was now 2003.

We walked into the tent to wash up. Nat looked the TA lad up and down as he dried himself from a cold shower.

"What's your nickname?" Nat asked him. He dropped his towel.

Rob Wills shouted "There you go, you will now be known as 'rat's cock', on account of a very small penis!"

Poor bastard; one minute a chemist at home, the next in a tent in Iraq with a load of maniacs staring at your manhood and renaming you 'rat's cock'.

8. Welcome To Iraq

A week later we boarded the Hercules airplane and headed North for Amarah, where the Euphrates River meets the Tigris River and formerly a key trading area for fish from the marshlands. A population of 1 million mainly Shia faith dominated the area. The British were held up there during the Great War of 1916 and many British soldiers were killed in the advance to Turkey. Now it was 2003 and I had the feeling that we hadn't moved forward a great deal in the pursuit of peace.

Some historians believe this river junction is the cradle of civilisation and the heart of Babylon. Now we were here, a modern day crusade sent by Tony Blair to deliver his idealist new world order.

We arrived at Amarah's Sparrowhawk Airport. There was no one to meet us, no ammo, no armoured warrior tanks, and we had no idea where we were or what to do should we be attacked. It was a complete logistical fuck-up. Good job Saddam wasn't ready to unleash an attack.

As the Hercules turned around for its returning flight, the fire brigade arrived escorted by a Land Rover.

"Quickly gents" an officer shouted, "head over to the blown up building before something kicks off"

This went against everything we had ever been taught; the IRA always placed bombs, IEDs and booby traps in derelict buildings because they are often used by soldiers as shelter from weather. But our odds of survival while standing exposed on a flat runway were probably even worse so we headed for the building. Some clever bastard had sprayed on the outside 'Club 18-30 Iraq Holidays'

. Inside there was rubble everywhere where a US Military guided missile had gutted it out, probably to stop the enemy using it for strategic purposes.

"Welcome to Iraq Airways!" Whatty laughed, putting his thumbs up to my camera. Whatty was only about five foot tall and had a strong Bristol accent, but he was a tough little fucker who probably wouldn't think twice about glassing you in the face if you made a remark about his height.

A Warrior turned up with my good friend Snips commanding it. I asked him, in my own way, what the score was;

"When are we getting picked up and taken to camp, piss-nuts?!"

"Fuck off lizard lips, it's not my fault, it's the handover from the Jocks. Their admin's up their ass so we're waiting on a vehicle to get you out of here. Camp's about two miles, if that, that way" he said, pointing behind me. I thought, 'you're joking, it's that close? We've been here an hour now!' It became clear that this operation was ill-prepared from the start. It was only at that point that two four-tonne vehicles finally turned up to take us to camp.

***

We got into camp Abu Naji by the afternoon and settled in to our 12 men tents.

"Not the mortar proof accommodation that we were told about." Caz said to me. We dished out ammunition and the new gadgets the Government had provided us with but, as always, it was one between two.

A Scottish soldier poked his head into our tent and asked if we wanted some buckshee ammo. I leapt from my bed.

"How much have you got, fella?" I asked enthusiastically.

From all the boxes he had I took an extra two magazines' worth, and so did the other guys. This by all accounts is completely illegal. We had only been issued four magazines, equalling 150 bullets each to protect ourselves with.

This was no place for rules. I wanted to survive; if the government wouldn't provide then I would.

***

The tour was slow and tedious, nothing but a few town raids and distribution of wind-up radios, a gift from the West as the town had no electric. They had a corrupt police force, no jobs and complete breakdown of infrastructure. But at least they had wind-up radios.

We promised so much but delivered very little. It was left up to 100-strong Companies to employ Western democracy to marshland tribes that had fought tribal battles for centuries. We were completely out of our depth. But Tony Blair ignored the signs and was happy to carry on dictating spin to the public in pure ignorance.

So the plan was to go to every village and do what we did in Sierra Leone; have an arms amnesty and remove their weapons from their homes, allowing one AK47 rifle and one magazine to each household.

But this was the Middle East, where they'd lived like this for hundreds of years; it would be like going to homes in England and demanding all of the TV's in the house.

***

The time was 10am and it was a wet and shitty morning. We were providing support on the outside of the village. Browny and I moved into the village as back up after the CSM and Major Pearce asked me to cover the south end of the building.

I had eyes on the CSM as he entered the town Sheikh's building for a meeting and I saw some movement at the back of the mud hut. As I moved closer, I saw the muzzle of a weapon.

"Stop fucker!" I yelled. Browny and I immediately cocked our weapons and moved in swiftly. The man dropped the weapon after a second aggressive challenge. The CSM froze and we kept our weapons trained aggressively on our target until Major Pearce walked calmly around the building and made us back off and move back onto the road.

"Well done you two, fucking shit myself then" said the CSM, "Thought he was going to get me!"

***

Three days later Sergeant Johnson received a radio message saying that the OC's Rover group had been involved in a massive fire fight down the road.

"Let's go — Webby you take your team's wagon and let's head to the next village down from Camp Condor."

As we got closer to the village it was clear that the battle was still on. A Chinook was circling overhead while Mac the medic was stood with a pile of three Iraqi bodies at his feet. A small crowd was gathering.

"Right Webby; me and you will move up the river bank" said Jono. "DA Borb's and Bobby Moore, take the rest of the blokes and set up an ICP and get those bodies covered up."

I was buzzing — this was more like it! As we patrolled slowly up the river bank towards the gunfire, Jono moved through the small mud huts and a woman came nervously out of her house.

"Ali Baba, Ali Baba?" I said quietly, using gestures to ask her which way the bad guys went. She pointed down away the river bank where we were heading.

Keeping as low as possible I could see that the river went on for miles and I noticed Jeck Hyde coming down completely out of breath, his hands shaking with adrenaline. The CSM ran

up to us and slipped on a new magazine. He was buzzing too. They had obviously just seen some action.

"Fucking hell Webby son, you would have loved that!" he said. I was gutted to have missed

it.

Major Pearce was controlling things from the ICP.

"Right, Mac and Jono, I want to get these bodies back in the town to the Red Cross centre and then get the fuck out of here before we end up like the RMPs" he said.

As we moved into the town a massive crowd had gathered and were throwing rocks at us. I turned to the interpreter, Asad, and asked what they were saying.

"They want to behead all of us" he replied.

"I don't think they want us here" said Benny, stating the obvious.

"Webby, over there — that kid's got a grenade!" shouted Asad pointing to a small youngster. I trained my weapon on the youngster and told him to put it down but he held it tight and moved behind a wall.

"I fucking mean it — imshee, imshee!" I yelled.

Now my weapon sight is on this kid's head and I'm thinking, do I shoot or don't I shoot? While I'm internalising this moral dilemma, I'm simultaneously scanning the area for places to take cover from the blast he could cause.

"Boss, this is Webby; we've got a very angry crowd out here, some of them with grenades" I said on the radio.

"Okay, we're going now... just giving them the final body" was the casual reply.

"Mount lads, let's get the fuck out of here. Well done Asad" I said as I trained my rifle on the wall where the kid went.

What if I had shot that child with the grenade? How would the public have judged me?

These are the difficult decisions soldiers face every day.

9. The Brecon Sniper

Two weeks later I was leaving Iraq to go on a course. It was a week before Christmas and nothing was happening in Amarah, so I thought 'bugger it, I'll get promoted quicker if I get this course out the way'. I went to the UK for a week of R and R before starting the course at Brecon. It was in Senny Bridge, Wales and a proper dog shit course in my opinion — they treated me like a dick from day one.

I had just been given an early promotion to full Corporal due to my qualification as a mortar fire controller. This course was seen as an extra qualification I could use to train recruits. The only reason I was up for it was because I wasn't seeing much action in Iraq. The tour was due to finish in April so as things stood I would not have to return afterwards. The problems there had effectively been solved... or so the politicians would have us believe.

I got off the plane at Brize Norton and whilst still in desert uniform ran out of the airport and got into the hire car I had booked. No weapon, no boundaries, no restrictions.

I spent a few days in North London with a girl I was seeing and after a great weekend there I headed for Falmouth. I could have gone out to my house in Spain, but I'd had enough hot weather — and after three months in Iraq, you just can't beat Cornwall.

It felt really good to cross the Tamar Bridge and go home, but when I got into my room that night and switched on the TV there were images of riots and turmoil in Amarah.

I couldn't believe my bad luck — here's me on a course learning about fighting and killing with weapons while my mates are out in Iraq doing the real thing. Things had changed out there and I wanted a piece of the action again. I needed a way out of the course and decided which card I would play... my old back injury.

I genuinely had damaged my back on Special Forces selection on the Brecon Hills a year previous. But it hadn't been giving me much trouble so I had to bluff it a bit to get off the course and out to where the real action was.

When I got back to Brecon I rang the Army movements clerk and provisionally booked a flight out to Iraq. That morning we were out on a run where I had planned to feign injury, but with about three miles left to go my back genuinely clicked out of place like a gift from the gods. That was the meal ticket that I needed just at the right time — there probably wouldn't have been much war left to fight otherwise.

"Get your ass up there you weak cunt!" screamed the instructor in my ear. I ignored him and completed the next lap around camp. As I neared the medical centre I slowed to a walk.

"Where the fuck are you going?!" he screamed again. The jumped-up git was only one rank above me. He was a Skill at Arms Instructor, generally known in the Army as a 'range Nazi' or 'health-safety pen-pusher.'

I strutted into the Medical centre. The doctor took one look at my medical history and put me on rehab back in Germany. 'Thanks doc,'

I thought, 'that will do me nicely.' I took my sick chit and gave it to my instructor and that was me out of there. I couldn't wait to get back to Iraq.

***

The next morning, after a brief on the next part of the course which I didn't listen to, I headed out that door for the last time. My mate Mickey Dimmock, a top lad and very much on my wavelength, said to me as I left "I will be following you out of here soon… won't be long before the Brecon sniper takes me out."

On that note I drove out of Brecon Camp bound for Iraq via Germany.

10. Return To Iraq

I was stuck on the Antwerp ring road when a text message came through on my phone from my mate Sturgy;

'Mate, things are kicking off again in Iraq, Natty and Wardy are injured, Harrison has been shot in a small village, they're desperate for replacement commanders'

This was bad news — my mates were hurt. The fighting he was referring to has since been widely written about and is referred to as the Battle of Qal At Salih. A Military Cross was won there.

I also got the message that 'Fingers' Windsor had been killed in a road traffic accident there a few weeks earlier. He was a nice lad from my platoon and a great loss to us.

To any sane person it may have seemed that I had picked a bad time to go out, as things were getting hectic, but this was exactly the reason I had blagged coming back and I was excited to get stuck in.

I was flying from Hanover direct to a secret American airbase in the Middle East. During the flight, it suddenly dawned on me that nobody knew I was coming back out — I was supposed to be on this course, but had effectively signed myself off and booked my own flight back out without telling anyone. When I got to Basra I would be on my own with no transport arranged to drive me the four hour trip to Camp Abu Naji in Amarah.

We arrived at the airbase where a Hercules plane would take us the rest of the way. We boarded at about 8pm and I noted that the atmosphere was very different to the last time I was there — you could sense the danger through the area's state of alert. It was a lot different to the cosy Argentina Airways arrival in October 2003. Now we were aboard an armed-to-the-teeth Herc with a door gunner hanging out the side. As we approached Basra airport the interior lights went out and we began a steep tactical land. For sure 2004 was going to be very, very different.

After a short briefing I still needed to sort out transport to Abu Naji. I saw some REME soldiers preparing their four ton vehicles to head out of the airport. I approached the nearest one, a big lump of a bloke.

"Where you heading mate?" I asked as he mounted his wagon.

"Abu Naji" he told me.

"Can I sponge a lift?"

"Where's your weapon?"

"I'm not supposed to be out here. But since you're driving, maybe I could use yours?"

"Help yourself, mate."

I looked to the back seat where his SA80 lay. It was covered in crap, had no magazine and hadn't even been oiled. This guy obviously wasn't too worried about getting ambushed during his drive on the notorious Route 6. For both our sakes, I started cleaning and sorting out the weapon as we headed north.

The road was dead and the driver briefed me up as I sat forward, staying alert in case of attack. Every 5 minutes I consulted my GPS so that I had an idea of where we were. This guy had no radio or fuck all, just a big bag of doughnuts. If we got hit I was ready for anything but he was acting like he was delivering rubber dildos to an Iraqi porn dealer. I was probably more of a godsend to him than he was to me.

I was a very paranoid individual and found it hard to relax. Perhaps it was my oversensitive nature that attracted negative situations.

Bizarrely, as we pulled into camp at Abu Naji it felt like I was coming home.

"Thanks mate, good luck" I said, laughing, to the driver.

I headed down to the tents. It was about 3am and no one was about. The only tent that wasn't locked was full to the brim with blokes so I put out my sleeping bag and got my head down in the corridor.

***

"Alright Webby, what are you doing here you mad bastard?" said Browny, spotting me lying like a maggot in the corridor, "Does Rob Warne know you're here? Since he's been in charge things have really changed."

Rob was a friend of mine, so I went to his tent to see him and there he was; a monster of a man sat relaxing in a way that reminded me of lions you see on wildlife programmes, lazing in the sun while the females hunt for dinner. He was sat on a deck chair wearing bright yellow shorts and covered in baby oil to improve his golden tan.

He took off his Oakley shades and this big smile appeared.

"Well helllooow! I thought you were on Brecon? Oh let me guess, the Brecon sniper, Spanish Mountains?" he laughed, "Good to have you out here mate, but you've missed the party. It was fucking fruity, we're lucky to be alive. I can't wait to get out of here now — me and Major Pearce have got a bounty of 500 fatwas and 10 goats on our heads"

"That's not a bad bounty mate, I might have a crack myself!" I joked as we moved into his tent and sat by his bed space.

Rob shared the tent with another Sergeant Major. While we were in there catching up, he walked in and looked me up and down, before walking out in apparent disgust. The reason for this, I believe, is that he saw that I was merely a Corporal.

This might seem odd, but anyone who has served will know how rank can change a person. You're not supposed to be close to someone who is a higher rank than yourself, but Rob Warne never changed one bit and always treated me the same as when we had first met. It didn't matter if you were a General or a week one private; that's just the way he is and the reason why he was loved by his men yet disliked by many of his peers.

"So you don't want any more riots or fire fights?" I said. Rob explained:

"Do I fuck! We've been confined to camp anyway due to the bounties. We went into Qalat Salih to do a regular patrol. Me and Dave Drummond wanted to search the police station and Maj Pearce was outside. We took some of your mortar platoon for support and experience. The Iraqi police didn't want to let us search the upstairs rooms so Dave pushed them out the way and kicked the door in. The floor was scattered with rocket propelled grenades and AK47 assault rifles, stolen from the locals ready to be sold to local bandits."

I asked how the Iraqi police had felt about it.

"What do you think? They went fucking mental as everything we taught them had gone out the window. We arrested two men and went out to see Maj Pearce and the mood of the whole village had completely changed.

Some policemen suddenly opened up on us from the station's entrance so we gave chase back into the building. I shot the flip-flop directly in front of me inside, but didn't see the one hiding to my left. Luckily Dave did and filled him with bullets. Then we heard small but weighty objects being rolled down the stairs... they were grenades.

"I pulled Dave out of the way as they went off, and he caught some shrapnel in the ass!" said Rob laughing. He was telling the story with such charisma it made me wish I had been there.

"We shot fuck out of the roof above us to kill the guy upstairs, then ran up there and finished the dude off. All hell broke loose as the town on the other side of the river let rip on us. The rest of the blokes had to make their way inside because they blew up our vehicles with RPGs. This is where I had to start turning the police station into a fortress... it was like at the end of the movie Young Guns, when they're trapped in the building, scared but buzzing at the same time!

"I met a PWRR Sergeant and his team who had come to help us from Camp Condor. He had been shot in the hand and Pte Harrison had been shot in the ass, and Nat caught some shrapnel in the bum too. I said to him, 'they couldn't miss your fat ass!'

"There was a couple hours of intense fighting. I was worried for the night time operations and ammo was running low so we dished out the AK47s and RPGs.

"Then the police phone started ringing in the building. I picked up and some cunt on the other end was talking shit, so I got the interpreter to take the call. They said if we did not surrender we would die like dogs, and reminded us of what happened to the RMPs up the road at Majar al Kabir. 'Right', I said, 'Tell that smelly prick I want 15 pepperoni pizzas and extra cheesy garlic bread'!"

I could not stop laughing because I knew him so well that I could imagine him saying it. No CSM would have handled the situation in such a way other than this crazy bastard.

I asked how the lads had been and he told me of their bravery — Harrison, Wardy, Natty, Dave Drummond and Ross Strick had all done themselves proud.

"The PWRR Sergeant kept firing even with a finger missing. Becky the clerk bagged a few as well" he said excitedly, "We called it FSP Company rinsing and you missed the party man. Only scraps left now."

"I can't believe it… sounds amazing Rob" I said.

"But that's it for me. I've a year left in the Army. I just want to get out of here now"

I asked what it was like when Fingers died. Rob's eyes filled with regret.

"Awful… never had to pack up one of my blokes' kit before. That's horrible, seeing pictures of his kid and his family, never want to do that again. We'll give him a FSP send off when we get back to Germany."

I walked out of the tent, picked up my kit and went to find Jono so I could get a bed space and a job role. I was blown away by Rob's story, and happy to be out there.

11. Story Of A Blown Up Soldier

Back in camp Abu Naji the rumour control going around camp was that Cpl Holmes's section had been involved in an explosion a week earlier. Holmes was getting a lot of negative vibes from the blokes who thought he was at fault. As he was one of my friends I wanted to hear the story from him, so I visited him while he was recovering at the medical centre.

Over a cigarette outside the med center he told me about what had happened.

"Why did you leave camp without a radio and communications?" I asked him, trying to be tactful.

"You know when you were down the town getting hammered during the riots? Well, we had to re-supply you lot by doing shuttle runs to and from Abu Naji. A young officer needed escorting down to CIMIC-House. My platoon Sgt was out at the time and had all the radio equipment on his wagons, leaving just two land rovers to deploy.

"Me and my team pleaded with the ops room, saying that it was dangerous driving through town, but the Captain just said 'get on with it' as it was imperative this fudgepacker of an officer got to CIMIC-House. As if the operation would be doomed to failure without another jumped-up university wanker causing problems!"

"So you were ordered to leave camp?" I asked. He nodded.

"I contested it and was not happy with leaving without a radio but we had to just get on and do it. I wish now I told them to fuck off but hindsight is a wonderful thing.

"So there we were, five miles from Abu Naji heading towards the first police check point near the built up area of Amarah. When we got there, I just remember the glass on the front window turning brown like it was all in slow motion... then it shattered into a million pieces. It felt like warm rain was landing on me and I was in a daze.

"I drew my rifle and tried to exit the wagon by the side. By now I was on auto pilot, just running through the drill of getting away from the vehicle. I was waiting to hear gunfire but luckily they hadn't set up a killing zone for us."

"That was considerate of them." I said sarcastically.

"I've got ball bearings in my wrist and ass and as I'm getting out of the vehicle my body can't hold me up properly because all my muscle tissue is severed by the shrapnel. Tommo and Mouse were in a bad way — they had absorbed most of the blast on their side and were not responding to my shouting. An Iraqi policeman ran up and grabbed my arm to lead me away

from my men but I shouted 'fuck off, leave us alone!' I knew in the back of my mind that they were only 100 metres away and man that check point 24 hours. You're telling me they didn't see anyone setting up the claymore on the side of the road? They might have even done it themselves!

"Then I remember drifting in and out of consciousness as I lost more and more blood. I lay on the side of the road in the prone position to make less of a target. My arm was shredded and it felt like there was a hot poker on my ass. I reached down with my decent arm and could feel a hole the size of a cheeseburger!"

"So how did you get out of there?"

"Luckily Ginge Daniels just happened to be going that way or we would have bled to death. I remember Jeck had to keep waking me to keep me alive because I just wanted to sleep as the blood drained from my body. The next thing I knew I was in a hospital bed in Basra and lying in a row were me, Mouse and Tommo, who was covered in bandages.

"The doctor walked up to Tommo and told him, ever so calmly, they would have to remove his leg as there was so much damage. I just burst into tears and said sorry to him. He lay there and told me it wasn't my fault. We were all in a right mess. Mouse later went to another ward and we didn't see each other again. I blame myself…"

"Don't mate because you will never move on. You were ordered to drive out of camp. Even if you had a radio you should have been in a snatch, not a fucking Land Rover… and where was the ECM to protect you? Why isn't it being used out here now?" I was genuinely frustrated that they had been let down.

Holmes continued. "When I got back to camp last week the Sergeant Major called me into his office. He said that it was all my fault and I would never get promoted because of it.

I'm 31 now, done all my qualifying courses three times over up to the rank of Sergeant. But when I had an interview with the CO the other day and asked about my rank to Corporal, he laughed and told me I was 'on the sick'. I had been blown up and he said there were no available spaces for downgraded corporals. I couldn't believe it — that was from Terry Hilling."

I nodded my head. I actually got on quite well with Hilling, but it was a raw deal H was getting.

Blame is a heavy burden but the truth is that there is no right or wrong side for soldiers. They are thrown into very strange situations and the outcome is always the same; negative.

This time was no different. Two soldiers had visible physical injuries; all three had emotional injuries that would last forever.

12. King Of The Ring

The next morning I opened my eyes to see this massive figure stood over me. It was my mate Toddy.

"You would have loved it last week mate," he laughed, "what a hoot! It kicked right off, I tell you. Rob Warne has really pulled this Company together. Did you hear about Qalat Salih?"

"Yes I did thanks, now fuck off." I replied. I was gutted to miss it and didn't need anyone else rubbing it in. I was missing every row this Battalion got involved with.

Big Rob had introduced physical training every morning to bond the company. That morning we all had to assemble in the basketball court for a round of 'king of the ring', a game designed to psyche us up for battle where we would fight for possession of a full water bottle. To make it funnier we climbed on each other's backs — it was a massacre. I was on Browny's back and he's strong as an ox, but punches flew and anything went to get that bottle.

Colour Sergeant Head shouted abuse from the side while refusing to take part, threatening to punch his bloke's faces in when they fell off each other's backs. His men just bowed their heads in shame at this.

"Why don't you ask CSgt Head why he's not playing?" Rob Warne said angrily, astride Big Toddy like his steed. Everyone stared at Head, awaiting a reply.

"I'm injured aren't I? I'd kick all your heads in if I was playing" Head said nervously.

"Nothing to do with being a fat bastard then? Fucking weak prick" said Rob. Head, obviously intimidated, walked away.

"Maj Pearce wants that fat bully busted down to Sgt when we get back to Germany" Rob said. "He's jacked out of every job out here with his fake injury and all of his blokes are scared of him. I'm going to kick his ass at some point."

***

That evening as we prepared to relieve the guard I noticed a lot of my multiple were acting a bit funny with me because I had been promoted and was away for seven weeks of the tour. They were obviously tired and pissed off from being on guard's duty in the watch towers, but I was enthusiastic and wanted to implement changes to their routine.

I figured it was about time they had a break, so asked Bobby Moore, one of the corporals, what was happening;

"What's the sketch on guard, Bobby?"

"Well mate, as commanders we sit in here and check IDs on the flip-flops coming in to work on the camp, book in patrols, and load and unload the men." he said.

I asked how many sangars there were and who would relieve them for a break during rotation. The reply was 'no one.' Apparently, even though our multiple had more corporals than privates, they thought they were too high a rank to do a job they considered boring and menial.

I always believed in leading by example — that's the way I was as a young commander and that's the way I was now I was a full Corporal. I would never ask my men to do anything I wasn't prepared to do myself, so was about to give these corporals a reality check. I walked into the guard room where they were all chilling out and reading magazines. I knew they had a problem with me so I thought I'd see how far I could push it.

"When are you going to relieve Ratman from Sangar 1?" I asked Steve Dobson.

"I'm going nowhere son, I'm sitting here and smoking some fags" he jeered.

I looked around at DA Blackwell, who was the main Corporal and acting Sergeant. He was also sat smoking a fag. Bobby was flicking him childishly.

"So let me get this straight..." I said, and pointed to them in turn, "one, two, three... oh, and me; that's four corporals sat in here scratching our bollocks while they stand watch for eight hours. When do we come off so they can have a rest?"

"At 07.00 tomorrow when we go on air reaction force" Bobby said.

"So what happens if we get called out to an incident tomorrow?"

"Well that's their tough shit!" Dobson said, "Listen, Webby — you can't come back from your nice little holiday and tell us what to do."

Bobby nodded his head in agreement. DA Blackwell leant back and said;

"Webby that's how it is — deal with it."

As he said this, I slipped a magazine onto my rifle before violently cocking it and pointing it at them. They all shifted back in their chairs uneasily.

"This is where I stand you bunch of cocks!" I seethed, "How about I kill all of you and then I'll run the show? Dobson, get your kit on and get your ass up to Sangar 1 in two minutes flat, you little red ass! Who the fuck do you think you are?!"

I ended up winning that little debate and things turned out differently than planned that night; the blokes all got a chance to relax in the guard room and I got to go up in the sangar with my gun, which was the best chance I was going to get to kill someone.

Ask any private soldier that served with me; I always did what the rest of the lads had to do and stayed on in the sangars. Shelly and Liam were the only other corporals I knew of who did this — the rest just sat back and let their blokes get tired. In my eyes this was not the best way to lead.

The next morning I overheard Benny and Bobby in the multiple moaning about my attitude.

"Listen lads," I said angrily, "there's no debate about this. I don't like this jack attitude in the group, get rid of it or I'll smash your faces in! You know I'll do it!"

Bobby was clearly nervous. "What have I done?!" he stammered.

"Take responsibility or I will sort you out!" I yelled.

I didn't handle this situation the best way and I'm sure I was a complete asshole to work with. But the only way I knew to solve problems was with violence. Or at least threats of violence.

I went and saw Sgt Johnson and said "Stick me in another team mate, otherwise I'm going to end up killing one of these."

"You can go out with Cpl Bridges' team to the Iranian border." said Johnson.

I acknowledged gratefully.

13. Mass Graves

We headed out to the Iranian border under the cover of darkness with a week's worth of supplies. We knew very little of the situation but we would be briefed by A Company on the handover as they had been there for a week so far. We heard rumours that Kuwaitis were looking for the mass graves where their relatives and loved ones had been buried. That didn't seem to make sense when we arrived and saw the area; it was a very open, flat spat of land that showed no signs of disruption.

There was a full moon and everyone was in high spirits because we were getting away from Camp Abu Naji. We set up camp as the petrol generator chugged away. Keo was making us all laugh with this stupid helmet he had on and proclaimed himself 'porn trooper' while wearing a jock strap and holding a dildo in his hand, jumping around like a court jester. Remember, we were on the border to Iran — if the Iranians had been spying on us they would have probably laughed their asses off.

In the morning I got up before sunrise to have a scout around the area and layout of the camp. The sun came up to the east and the view was tranquil and calm. I can remember thinking, 'how can there be such glory in such a negative place?'

Then I remembered that this was supposed to be Babylon; where writing was invented, the beginning of civilisation. That's when I realised how truly beautiful this country was.

As this thought crossed my mind, Private Prosser came up to speak to me. I had recruited him to join the Light Infantry — he was Welsh and a really friendly chap.

"Bet you Support Company lot brought deck chairs so you could top up your tans!" he joked.

"Fuck off, we had to dig in and patrol every two minutes" I responded, "You're in the wrong platoon for that shit, Taff!"

He died a few weeks after we returned home from Iraq. He was attacked by some thugs in Wales, hit his head and went to sleep. Bless his soul — he was a great soldier with huge potential.

***

We had a brief and set up the camp deck chairs and radio to establish communication with camp Abu Naji. The TA captain in charge of us looked like Chevy Chase and was quite intimidated by the experienced soldiers he was in charge of, but he was doing all right for a bank manager.

Our mission was to provide security for the camp and carry out regular patrols to the border and back with the Land Rovers.

"So why are the Kuwaitis here, sir?" Ross asked the boss.

"During the war in 1991 when Saddam invaded Kuwait, any Kuwaitis found in Iraq as they advanced were taken to the border and shot. Some were buried alive... men, women and even children. This is one of the reasons we're here, to protect the Kuwaitis looking for their loved ones' remains. Hundreds were killed out here." he said.

A Kuwaiti man approached us and told us that they had captured an Iraqi bus driver who witnessed the acts, and they were threatening to kill him so he would confess where the bodies were buried. It was going to be like looking for a needle in a haystack; it had happened 11 years ago and the Iraqi might say anything with a gun to his brains.

We all watched as they frog marched the Iraqi man to the area. He was understandably terrified as the Kuwaitis began to lose their tempers. There were diggers and dumpers with the engines running, ready to begin the search. This was a very tense situation.

A big Kuwaiti who had hold of the Iraqi lowered the gun from his head and marched him back to the range rover. The man had his head in his hands as the diggers went to work, as if he had cleared his conscience. At this point Rob Warne and Maj Pearce turned up to assess the situation and deliver rations and mail.

"No way are they going to find anything here." Big Rob said.

"Yeah, I don't fancy their chances" I agreed, "How's things back in camp?"

"Not good. The PWRR haven't been briefed very well and are asking to borrow lots of our kit because they haven't brought any. They are in shit order. Our officers are walking around camp with fuck all to do but pick you up for not wearing your beret." he answered.

When a Major and a CSM with bounties on their heads are coming out on a ration run, you know it must be shit back at camp.

***

The next day a Kuwaiti approached us with a video camera and announced "Today is great day!"

"Why?" I asked him.

"Because we find our remains today and without your help we would not have accomplished this mission" he said.

We all rushed over to see the events unfold as they discovered body after body. There were skulls everywhere. Some of the bodies had their hands tied behind their backs. Some had been shot, others buried alive. We weren't taking it that seriously until we saw the remains of children — a horrific sight.

One of the lads summed it up; he simply said, "Why?"

They gave us a flag to celebrate with them and we asked how many were pulled out of the ditch. The man replied sadly;

"80 bodies... Mothers, fathers buried with the children."

He thanked us and walked over to the ditch and started placing out serial numbers for the corpses. We put the flag down after our photo opportunity and looked at the faces of the Kuwaitis. They looked content. Before this I had mixed views about Saddam Husain and wondered if a lot of his reputation was down to media spin and propaganda. But this really hit home. He had effectively committed all these murders by giving orders to ethnically cleanse the Kurds and Kuwaitis.

I had witnessed it firsthand. But it just left me with more questions: Are the Iraqis barbaric people? Are we crusaders using democracy to cover up greed?

What defines evil? Did that Iraqi man have to clear his conscience to move forward in his life? Who would judge him, and what would be the consequences for his acts? Would I be like him once the war was over? Would the demons in my head remind me of what I had done and seen and the power I perhaps had to stop these acts from happening? Who would judge the dictators and politicians that never had to bear witness to the orders carried out? And who would judge me for what I had let happen in operational theaters?

Who knows… but the world is one fucked up place and there are some very evil people on this planet.

14. Calm Before The Storm

Rob Warne had arranged a curry night as a treat for the lads and that afternoon we handed in all our trace rounds, night sights and riot gears. These were telltale signs that we would be leaving Iraq and the PWRR advance party was getting settled in for a long six month tour. I was a little disappointed that nothing was kicking off having made such an effort to get back out there. I felt like the best opportunities to get involved had passed me by, including Qalat Salih.

Big Rob was dishing out cans of beer to the lads and the curry was NATO-standard stink rustled up by some greasy slop-jockey who looked just thrilled to be having his evening spoiled by a rowdy mob like us.

Maj Pearce was in fine spirits, remarking on the tour in good humour. RSM Bob Dunstan joined us for a beer and even when the CO walked in the mood was good.

Suddenly, there was a huge boom which made the RSM jump with fright. Everyone burst out laughing, knowing that it was an outgoing mortar — Recce were calling in mortar illumination on a potential target to scare them away. Some fucked up tactic created by Whitehall. The RSM went bright red and said, "That scared the shit out of me! You could have warned me you bastards!"

But our fun was cut short; Maj Pearce put down his beer and announced: "The curry night's off. Go and re-draw all the riot kit and night sights. Be ready to move on the wagons for 19.00. It's kicking off down town and A Company are surrounded at CIMIC-House."

"Wankers," said Nat, "let's get down there and sort them out. Fucking ruin my curry night!" Always thinking about his guts, the fat bastard.

***

With the engines running and everyone eager to join the action, we were ready to kick some ass. Off we rolled into the night. I had never been into the town before — they had Warriors lining the route on all flash points like cross roads and bridges.

After Maj Pearce met with John Proctor, a commander struggling to establish order in the town centre, it became clear that the situation had died down so we returned to camp. The OC gathered us in and explained that A Company had coped with the public disorder tonight but the local Sheikhs and tribal leaders were going to stage a demonstration tomorrow. We were to support A Company and were told to be prepared to stay at CIMIC-House government building for a few days.

That night as we tried to sleep, the heaviest storm I had ever heard pounded our tents. It was a sign from the gods — something felt like it was going to kick off big time.

15. Good Day's Shooting

The next morning when we walked out to go to scoff we saw the effects of the previous night's storm; the soil was a deep blood-red colour having soaked up the night's hatred and seemed very symbolic of the rebels' feelings towards the infidels. It probably was just the stale rain, but it had left that pungent smell in the air as if this day would be a bad one.

We mounted our wagons and did our final kit checks. Jono handed in the flap sheet to take to the ops room and we were then ready to deploy. Rations got dished out, which meant the intelligence was good; they knew we weren't going to solve this problem in a day. My Granddad always said it wasn't a good sign when you're given food — it means they want one last big push.

I had only been to the centre of Amarah at night, so I was quite looking forward to this mission. Little did I know of the impact it would have on my life.

We headed into the unknown, apprehensive about what lay ahead. The Warriors had lined our route in for our protection because Land Rovers wrapped in chicken wire don't stop RPGs, no matter what some punk politician says.

As we moved near the town centre we could hear sporadic gun fire. It turned out to be coming from one of the Warriors — my mate Oddy was returning fire at a small group of militia who were trying to take out a land rover with an RPG.

We entered CIMIC-House. The gates opened and I was looking up at this gigantic water tower that A Company were protecting. Just before the gates shut, Lamby and Browny pointed out the Pink Palace.

"That's where we were fighting at Christmas, Webby... that's the Tigris River, and that's Tigris Street where all the riots will take place later" said Browny as he pointed at various landmarks. "This is CIMIC-House... There's an empty swimming pool inside. It's handy, good for all our kills.

"You see that floating bridge down Tigris Street that crosses the river? That's where Fingers got killed, poor bastard. And what were the locals like when he died? Laughing and chucking stones, the fucking stinking flip-flops" he said angrily, "but what do you expect from primates?"

***

Bobby Foden, the OC's signal man, was hearing from intelligence reports of other Warrior call signs that large numbers of protesters were gathering outside — approximately 500 strong and gaining.

"Hmm, not bad odds..." he joked.

Without warning the front gate burst open and Oddy and his team dragged in a corpse — the first catch of the day. At first everyone stared in amazement before starting a slow clap which built to applause. Oddy took a bow before walking over to us, cool as a cucumber.

Oddy was great fun to be around and a first rate soldier, although sometimes his mad sense of humour led him to be underestimated. He had missed out on a 'Mention' in dispatches from the invasion of Iraq.

"Right lads, the boss said put him in the swimming pool. Sorry Webby but that little bastard was waiting for you lot… we came round the corner and he was there pointing his RPG at the road — but his luck just ran out! Ha ha ha!" he cackled.

At that moment a snatch vehicle came roaring through the gates and screeched to a halt as the commander, a soldier known to us as Creature, climbed from the side. He opened the back doors and two dead Iraqis slumped out, limp as noodles. They reminded me of a couple of Saturday night drunks, only they were covered in blood with their faces shot to pieces.

"Good day's shooting, well done lads!" Creature said.

The RSM approached the vehicle and told the two young lads inside to get out. As they did, empty bullet cases came pouring out and the smell of congealed blood and cordite hit our senses. The young pair braced up to attention for the RSM thinking they would get a telling off for killing people. They were visibly shaking from the adrenaline.

"Well done you two. How long have you been in son?" the RSM asked.

"Two weeks" one replied.

"Fuck me, two weeks in battalion and you got two confirmed kills?!" added the RSM, like it was a good thing.

Creature pulled a wounded survivor from the rear of the vehicle and dropped him into the medical wagon. The man could not stand because his bollocks were hanging off and he was going into shock with the pain. We all peered in to have a look at his wound as Bobby Bits, the medic, tended to him. It didn't take long for the amount of patrols coming in with Iraqi casualties to increase. 'How long will it be before we start getting killed?'

I wondered.

***

We put on our riot kit around dinner time and as we peered over the camp fence we saw a massive crowd of people building down Tigris Street who were chanting and attacking the palace.

Major Pearce briefed us on our task;

"Right gents, close in. Soft posture, non-aggressive, riot shield hidden and floppy hats, not helmets. We don't want to antagonise them. Their aim is to take the palace because of the lack of jobs and the poor infrastructure we have established"

Rob Warne was swinging his double clubs about and flicking out kung fu kicks, saying "If the crowd wants to dance they will be sorry!"

OC John Proctor overheard and approached him.

"I don't want no trouble here… I know how heavy handed Fire Support Company can be. Remember these are my people and we have an understanding down here."

"You fucking what?!" replied Warne incredulously, "I tell you what Sir, I'll mount up our wagons and you can sort this mess out, seeing as you've done such a good job! These aren't your people — they're bastards that want us dead, and if they want a scrap we won't stand back and let them dominate the ground — we will show them a hard time Sir!"

Proctor's face said it all — I got the strong feeling that he was out of his depth.

This was now our time to move and Jono called us forward to get into position on the side of Tigris Street and keep the riot shields low. The crowd was now 1,000+ strong and chanting aggressively.

We took the opportunity to sit down and chill out.

16. The Rules Of Engagement (The Yellow Card)

Before I go deeper into what happened in Iraq I need to give some perspective on how it differed to my previous tours…

It's easy enough to get into the Infantry, but you only become a true soldier once you've had that first operational experience. Northern Ireland is where I learned my trade; my survival in Iraq relied on fundamental skills and drills that kept me alive during the violence over there.

Following the many decades of conflict in Northern Ireland and with countless lives lost, Britain had established by the 1990's an excellent standard of soldier, designed to cater for civilians' needs and change their outlook on conventional warfare so that it was viewed more as urban peacekeeping.

First we were given a mission statement from the government at the time. Our mission was to assist the RUC to help restore peace and normality to Northern Ireland. We had the 'Northern Ireland Emergency Provisions Act'

, a soldier's bible which contained the rules for powers policing the province. Also in place was the yellow card, or Instructions For Opening Fire In Northern Ireland Code 70771.

This was issued with the blue card instructions for Making An Arrest In Northern Ireland Code 70772B

. These were read and recited daily by the troops in case of a situation.

In 1999 1st Battalion Light Infantry had just returned from a two year swan about in Cyprus (bloody good times, by the way). But when we returned to the UK we could not deploy on an operational tour until the unit had completed and passed battalion level training. We were told that we would be involved in the Drumcree marching season — this was expected to be the big showdown between Loyalist Orangemen and all those mad men in Portadown.

We underwent very intensive training for months at company level. In the summer that followed we went to the Northern Ireland training centre to do an intensive six week training package.

As you can imagine, that's a lot of training. We did various role plays and acted out scenarios to prepare ourselves. We were tested to the maximum and passed at a very high standard — so highly on the riot training, in fact, that FSP Coy had the Bridge on the first day of Drumcree.

***

Northern Ireland was also the first time I met Rob Warne. It was the year 2000 and my company were getting hammered by loyalist paramilitaries on the Drumcree Bridge, but after a while they got tired from pushing our six foot shields and calmed down, allowing us a short break. I told them I was a catholic and loved to sleep with their girlfriends while they were away causing bother. They hurled back lots of Bobby Sands jokes and we started to get on well for a while. I found the situation amusing, but all of a sudden the crowd started to go mad again — I didn't understand as it had seemed to be under control.

Then I heard this man behind me singing 'la la la la' and waving his hickory stick in the air like he was an orchestra conductor. He was a big bloke and doing this funny little skip-like dance. The crowd started shouting 'You fat bastard, you fat bastard.' But he just kept waving his stick and goading them to throw more stones. It was Sgt Rob Warne they were chanting at.

"Alright baked bean dick, what's the score?" said Rob, squaring up to the 1LI. It was all a bit much for the young officer who seemed intimidated, so I took it upon myself to take over the brief.

"Right Rob, this is easy; just try and make conversation with the rioters and calm them down."

With that, Rob walked up to the shield face-to-face with one of the biggest paramilitaries and said;

"Go tell 'Mad Dog' Johnny Adair I've just finished banging his mum up the arse!"

The crowd erupted and launched a massive cascade of boulders that bounced right off my helmet, nearly knocking me clean out.

"See you later mate" I said as I legged it away from the chaos with Liam, Ratman and Gibbo. I glanced back and saw Rob continuing to wave his stick and wind up some of the hardest men in the UVF, the crazy bastard. Four years later from that moment and many mad situations later, I'm sat there on a wall and waiting with that same crazy bastard to set up a base line.

This is how we operated. FSP Coy had previously been used at some serious public order events in Northern Ireland because of our controlled aggressive nature.

It suited the government then and it suited them now to use us for the Amarah situation, but using the same rules as were working under in Northern Ireland. This was doomed to fail. In N Ireland, we would be told where we were going, when, why, what we were going to do, and how we would do it, precisely… in Iraq, we were lucky if we were told one of those. We were out of our depth. Making up the rules on the spot wouldn't work, so instead they told us to use the yellow cards we already had. It was a shambles.

Amarah town's head police approached Jono. The crowd was building — possibly 2,000 strong by this point — but it was nothing we hadn't seen before. The Irish were the kings of rioting so we didn't expect the Iraqis to be a problem.

The stones being thrown went from pebbles to apple-sized rocks and ball bearings fired from catapults came shooting past.

"Helmets on, visors down, form a base line, hard posture!" Jono shouted, moving himself into position as the police officer tried to reason with the crowd.

As we established the line DA Blackwell got hit on the knee by a rock. It made a tremendous thud.

"Oof, you fucker, that hurt like hell!" Blackwell said. We all laughed. No one was scared as we had stood alongside each other to face countless public disorders in Northern Ireland and training. If anything it was quite exciting.

Now it was time to unleash a tirade of hell on these young and misguided Iraqis.

As I looked to my left, amid the chaos was a Northern Ireland snatch vehicle approaching. Now we felt at home. Behind that in two small columns was a snatch team ready to deploy into the hostile crowd.

17. How Snatch Works

The purpose of a snatch team is to stay hidden until the last minute before the baton gun is fired. Once a rioter has been shot and fallen in immense pain, the base line opens up just a fraction to let out four of your biggest, hardest men to grab the offender and drag him back behind the baseline. Then, if he's lucky, he's given tea and biscuits in the back of the snatch vehicle.

Well, that's what happens in training. In reality things are slightly different; when some Iraqi has been throwing grenades and blast bombs at you the rules change. Only the politicians don't seem to grasp this bit, and that's because they are totally unrealistic.

The crowd was getting closer to us. This is when you get problems. You need some sort of buffer zone.

"Adjust your visors, make sure your shields are down… Advance!" shouted Rob Warne as one of their grenades exploded nearby.

"Keep it together, keep it tight" I shouted to my team.

"Grenade! Over there on the left — Move back, move back!" Natty shouted as we all hastily shunted back dragging our heavy, cumbersome shields that would provide no protection from a bomb blast whatsoever.

Boom!

The second grenade went off. Now we had permission to fire the baton guns. We were allowed to shoot to kill now — the 'Rules Of Engagement' on the yellow card issued to soldiers states that you can do so if the enemy 'is committing or about to commit an act likely to endanger life, and there is no other way to prevent the danger.'

This is the rule of the yellow card, word perfect... for Northern Ireland. The only problem was that we were in Iraq. It was not 1996; it was 2004 and our Government had sent us to a foreign country with old, shitty equipment that had been designed for Northern Ireland. We were never given any proper training, a proper mission, proper rules of engagement or powers of arrest or advice manuals like the 'Northern Ireland Provision Act.'

No Arabic lessons for any of us, no grounding in the Arabic beliefs or cultures to help us understand Islam and these people and their ways a little better. They dropped us right in at the deep end and expected miracles.

It was now the afternoon and we had endured hours of Grenade attacks and being pelted with petrol bombs and stones. It was time to start pushing them back as the guys at the back gate were trying to stop some Iraqi teenagers from piling in and taking the palace from us.

"Baton gunners!" Andy Buller shouted from behind.

"Good to see you here!" I said, looking around at him.

His big eyes widened and he shouted, "Webster, face your front you Crowww!"

Liam was stood next to him and started laughing. Spence the baton gunner moved into position looking for one of the little bastards chucking grenades.

"There he is, engage now!" Jeck shouted. The shields opened for a fraction and little Spence, who was just 18, drew his rusty old 1950 baton gun and leaned forward to take the shot. Bang!

— the guy who was just about to throw a grenade at us fell in a heap on the floor clutching his wrist in agony.

The soldiers roared with rage, shouting abuse at the offender and praise to Spence who had just earned himself a few pints at the bar. Hilly shouted out "his hand is hanging off!" The Iraqi kids saw this and their side moved well back giving us a better tactical advantage. These Iraqis now knew we meant business and our morale was high. 'You're going to have to kill us all if you want to win that palace'

I thought. The lad with the hand hanging by a shred of flesh started to move back towards the elder men who had sent him to throw the grenade. It was clear that the elders were asking the youngsters to do all the fighting... but I suppose the same could be said with the British army recruiting soldiers as teenagers.

***

Before long we reached a stalemate on Tigris Street but the Iraqis weren't done — their next tactic was to send down a man who was showing signs of mental illness. He approached carrying a bag full of grenades and we could not see if the pins were in or out. This was the crowd taking full advantage of one of their own who clearly had a disability. I was shocked.

I looked to the roof and saw our 'eye in the sky' Trapper, who had his L96 sniper rifle well trained on the intruder. We all started to draw back, and there between the warring crowds was this simple soul sent by his own people with a bag of explosives to blow us all to Kingdom Come. "Back off now, back off now

dick head!" Rob Warne shouted, adding "Right, after three I want all the baton guns to fire around him."

Boom Boom Boom!

They sounded impressive but even the Iraqis could see that the guns had no effect. They started picking up the plastic bullets from the floor and throwing them back at us.

The guns, once you fired more than 20 rounds, became clogged with carbon and needed scrubbing out. As we stopped to do this, the man kept approaching. He had dropped the bag of grenades, but was now stooping to pick an unexploded one from earlier which had no pin. Everyone made ready — this was the only point all day that we had brought our main weapons to arm.

"Do not shoot him, do not shoot him!" Rob Warne shouted. "There are people through and beyond lads — do not shoot him!"

It says under the Rules of Engagement to 'kill to prevent a life threatening situation'. A lot of experienced soldiers had their fingers just itching to pull the trigger and end this poor guy's life, but no one fired. Why not?

Because Rob Warne said not to. He might have been mad in some people's eyes, but he is a very compassionate man. He would not admit it but he knew we would not achieve anything by killing him. Besides which, the man never got to within throwing range.

"Fatima Whitbread couldn't throw that grenade up here" Rob commented. The man eventually went back to the crowd.

At that moment the Iraqis started to disperse and head home as if it was their tea break. We withdrew into the Pink Palace, took off our helmets and watched the sun going down as if it would be our last sunset.

It was the closest time we'd come to using our rifles so far as a company. Finally we had a chance for action but it came to nothing. We were all in two minds; one was, 'we have spent years waiting to pull the trigger and end the enemy's life'

the other was, 'Northern Ireland taught us only to shoot as a last resort'

. But the bottom line was, if we had killed him, we would have been acting lawfully.

However, he was mentally handicapped, and it would have been morally wrong.

Can you see how confusing it was for us to fight two completely different wars, with completely different cultures and dialect, according to the precise same written rules? How could the Yellow Card possibly work in Iraq?

This was one of the government's critical errors. The poor planning of its misguided, illegal occupation is unforgivable.

18. Battle For The Pink Palace

"Webby, guess what? We got the roof tonight!"

"Yes! Get in!" I said nervously. This was exactly what I wanted to hear but we were all apprehensive, and the word from intelligence was that it wasn't going to be a picnic. We were still really tired from the day's riots and there was going to be no rest now. Little did I know of the life changing events ahead of us.

We heard the news stream over BFBS (British Forces Broadcasting Service) that the Italians had fled their Government building and it had been taken over by Sadr militia. This was a big political statement in Amarah; whoever dominated the Pink Palace and CIMIC-House appeared to have control of the city. It would be a disaster if they took those buildings and caused us to suffer casualties. It was imperative for us to hold both buildings and stand our ground at all costs. We were up for it... but so were the Mahdi Army.

Fire Support Company was solely involved because A Company could not handle the incoming fire and riots at CIMIC and the sports stadium. The OC of A Company was the most arrogant unapproachable man I had met in my career and the general opinion of Major Proctor's ability around battalion was as follows: listen to anybody else before listening to him.

It became really dark and claustrophobic in the compound of CIMIC-House. On the right hand side stood a seven foot wicker fence that hid a 50 meter river. Overlooking the wicker fortress was this enormous mound of reclaimed land, which was an ideal spot from which to launch a mortar attack, sniper or just cut us to pieces with RPGs and small arms fire.

Maj Pearce, Maj Proctor and the two Sergeant Majors had a second meeting to decide the plan of action for the next few days and nights from the back of a snatch wagon.

"What I want you to do is position your blokes around the Palace — we want no trouble round here — and in the morning we will relieve you. Come back here and get breakfast, and only fire if fired upon by militia." Maj Proctor said arrogantly.

"So basically," Rob Warne responded, "these ringpieces around CIMIC and the Palace want to flush us out and kill us if we don't hand over the building? Here's my answer to that; any dickhead that wants to dance with us will get slapped hard."

"No, no Sergeant Major, these are my people — I will not have you come down here and ruin our community relations with them!"

As if on cue, another explosion hit the perimeter fence. Big Rob said sarcastically, "Yeah Sir, you've done a great job building relations down here."

Proctor was obviously deluded if he thought he had control. This is why Saddam ruled so well because the only language these Iraqis seemed to understand was being ruled by an iron fist. Shit, I know, but that's how they live. And if you don't stand your ground against people like that, you will get your ass kicked.

Aggression and extreme violence was how we were going to deal with these pricks. Self-preservation and bringing every man home alive was our priority. If the British Government didn't like our tone then they were just as deluded as Maj Proctor was.

A Coy were in control of CIMIC and FSP Coy were in control of the Palace. That's 200 men with nine Warrior call signs on hand for armoured support. Amarah was about the same size as Plymouth so we had God knows how many militia to fight against.

There was the most almighty explosion as an RPG made a direct hit on the front gate, quickly followed by a rapid succession of small arms fire. A snatch wagon returning from a patrol started to engage the enemy, who were firing in short bursts from the top of Tigris Street. The snatch quickly sped through the gate before screeching to a halt and Big Rob went into gear.

"Right horse cocks, get all your riot kit with you and leave it in the palace compound. You can't get back here to get it tomorrow. Jono — load up your men and make your way over to the Palace. I want you in position by 19.00" he said before performing a familiar little skip and kicking his leg out. Everyone started to laugh.

As we loaded up in the sand pit we looked over at the snatch and saw my friend Creature and his men removing more dead enemies, rolling them down by the side of the wall. As I walked closer I heard "Give us a hand with this one Webby, he weighs a ton." So I helped drag his body to the side of the road and we left him there.

There was now quite a collection stacking up. One of the Iraqis was still alive and screaming in pain holding his stomach. A member of Creature's team propped his head up with a rucksack and opened his water bottle allowing the wounded man to take sips from it. It was a strange and profound moment of compassion that struck me as out of place. I couldn't help but wonder if we would have received the same treatment if we had been caught by them. I thought of what happened to those RMPs at Majar al-Kabir. Would we have been beheaded on some sick website like Ken Bigly and Nick Berg? I think we would have been tortured and probably killed in a very cruel way.

Bobby the Medic pulled his shirt up and revealed the wound where a bullet had skimmed his belly without entering and had opened him up like a surgeon's knife. His intestines were pushed out through the hole like a bag of sausages squeezed under intense pressure. You could see what he had eaten that day if you looked close enough.

"Right, well done lads, good day's shooting. Now let's go, let this lot sort these Iraqis out" Jono said. No sooner had the words left his mouth than we heard the snap, snap, snap

of gunfire over our heads — we were under attack.

19. Dance With The Devil

To our left, where the enemy fire was coming from, there was a tall metal fence which offered some protection, but there was nothing on the right to protect us from snipers. Our path back to the palace was also vulnerable.

There was a huge boom... the sound of an RPG hitting the wall of the compound.

"Two minutes, kit on and meet by the loading bay ready to move!" Jono shouted. We all reacted to his commands and I could feel the adrenaline start to pump around my body.

"Right," I said to my section, "grab your riot gear so we don't need to come back here tomorrow morning"

With a magazine of 30 rounds we loaded our rifles up and I could see the men were ready for it.

"You ready Webby?" said Jono.

"Yes, let's go" I replied.

By now it was dark. The riot gear we had with us didn't help our cover... the shields clunked noisily on the floor, breaking the ghostly silence of the night.

"Try not to drag your shields" I whispered back at Big Richie. The moon was bright and full above the Pink Palace we had to defend. They say people go mad during a full moon. We were about to find out if it was true.

"Webby, you and Browny check the perimeter of the palace and we will meet up in one hour on the roof top" Jono said. I acknowledged his order. The OC and Rob Warne were by the entrance to the palace and called us over.

"Alright, skip rat?" the OC said to me. I laughed at his mad sense of humour.

He turned to Jono: "After Webby's done his checks, move your guys up on to the roof and position them where you want — tonight is going to get lively."

With that Big Rob turned to the group and said: "Tonight, gents, we are going to dance with the Devil."

Boy was he right.

***

It was around 8pm and things had settled down. The rioters had probably gone for their dinner — after all, everyone's got to eat — but were definitely up to something. The town was deserted. I think they may have been broadcasting from their Mosques earlier telling the public to rise up against the infidels.

What you need to remember is we would have gladly not fired a single shot had they gone about their normal business. But they were trying to kick FSP Coy out of the building so that they could kill us and we weren't about to start waving white flags without retaliating. We were British soldiers.

Jono reminded me to keep an eye on the back gate as some kids had set fire to it earlier. I set off with Browny on patrol and we noticed two dodgy characters at the back of the palace in a dingy car lock. We had them in our sites and were ready to waste the motherfuckers.

Trapper was watching from the roof. One of the Iraqis was moving to the boot of his car and I had my site picture right on his head.

"Go on you bastard... pull an RPG out from that car, I fucking dare you!" Browny chuckled.

As he opened the car boot the other man handed him a radio which he placed inside.

"Damn it," Browny said, "I was sure they were dodgy!" We reported the incident over the radio and continued with our patrol.

Patrolling can be a boring job, so we were always eager to uncover some action. It was slightly disappointing that these men turned out to be acting innocently. But it didn't take long for some action to find us — we heard the high pitched 'zip'

that gunfire makes when the bullet passes your head at very close range.

We moved into cover and heard someone at CIMIC returning fire — the more standard 'bang bang'

that most people would identify as gun shots.

We couldn't be flippant with our bullets as we'd only been issued 150 rounds each and no tracers. Jono ordered us to move up so we headed for the roof.

We entered the building. Hiding inside like rats were the Iraqi police.

"What a surprise" I sighed. They knew that we were going to get shot to fuck that night. They had been tipped off that we were protecting the building and weren't going to step one foot outside of it.

"What's that, shimoolies?" somebody said as illumination rockets lit up the sky to make the enemies visible.

"No, that's 81mm mortar"

"Well I bet it's not our mortar platoon, you can see the cunts!" Rob Warne joked. Everyone burst out laughing.

"Sir, I've just done a perimeter check" I said.

"Well done, what do you want? A fucking Victoria Cross! Do you want me to suck you off?!" a sarcastic Big Rob replied. I should have known better than to feed him with ammo for piss-taking. He turned to address the group as a whole;

"Right lizards, pull up some chairs and get yourselves comfortable. Let me tell you a story of 50 tired, worn-out hard bastards with their backs up against a wall, cornered by Mr. Sadr's men. Do we want to dance? You bet your ass we do!" said Big Rob dancing around, again making us laugh. He continued: "Bring it on if you want to play with the big guns, bring it fucking on!"

Rob Warne's taste for battle was infectious. He had the blokes so fired up that we could take on any foe. He empowered his men, and that's what the ultimate leader does.

Me and Browny quickly climbed the stairs to the roof of the palace where I met up with Jono and got Trapper to keep an eye on those two dickheads in the car lot. An RPG came flying up Tigris Street with a 'whoosh'

and we all went to ground. It exploded at the Sangar of CIMIC-House.

From where we were, we could not see the enemy's firing point, so it was a case of crawling on our bellies and praying we weren't in a sniper's sights. Fire fights were breaking out all around, lasting a few minutes before stopping.

The OC joined us on the roof. I could hear every word that came through on his radio; it seemed that A Coy were getting involved in little battles all over the town. One of the young officers was trying to send his situation report and location status, something he had probably learned to do at Sandhurst, but he was totally out of breath and seemed to be struggling to concentrate while under fire. He said his call sign and I realised it was Creature's multiple — he was a Corporal with them.

"Calm down, calm down... send me your position when you have safely extracted your call sign from danger. Out!" said the OC, laughing at what the poor bastard was trying to do. But they survived.

"We need to be on that side of the roof, Jono" I shouted.

There was more zipping and snapping as bullets flew over our heads. We quickly got down on our belt buckles and crawled into the knee height wall line; the gunfire was everywhere, but no one could clearly identify the firing point so no one could fire a shot back.

"Get that GPMG over here now, Mac!" I said. "Over there, firing over there!"

"Be careful, this could be friendly fire. Don't fire unless you can clearly identify the enemy target, and all that rules of engagement malarkey" said Browny from beneath the hailstorm of bullets.

Earlier I had pressed record on my video camera, which was attached to my webbing straps. With all the action that had taken place since, I had completely forgotten it was rolling. You should see some of this footage in the film.

"What's that red light on your vest? Are you filming this?" said Head, who was crouched in a corner of the palace roof.

"Yes, it's a camera" I replied defiantly.

That man would never take his blokes on to the streets if there was a risk of hard work or danger. He said he had bad knees and wasn't allowed under doctor's orders, but seemed happy to take a senior rank's wage without doing his job.

20. Storm On The Roof

On the roof to one side there was a figure crouched motionless beneath a poncho.

"Who lives under there?" I asked Richie.

"That's Trapper" he said.

Trapper was our resident sniper, a Royal Green Jacket who had been up on the Pink Palace rooftop for three weeks under heavy gunfire. He'd been living on hard routine, eating cold rations, shitting in bags and pissing in bottles. The Royal Green Jackets were known as "chosen men". This guy was hardcore, no doubt about it. More bullets zipped past. I thought, 'where's that coming from now?' I saw a shadow move swiftly across the roof top. It caught my attention because it had no helmet despite being under sustained gunfire. It was Trapper on the move — you can't use an L96 sniper rifle's sight with the issued helmet because of its design.

So there was me, with my Army helmet done up as tight as I could get it, and there's this poor bloke with no protection.

***

"Right Webby," said Jono, "I want you to position your blokes down facing Baghdad Street. Push them out as quick as you can"

Behind me I heard a smoker's cough that I would recognise anywhere. It was Andy Buller.

"I couldn't sit back at HQ and put my feet up when the boys I trained are up here in the thick of it!" he said. He was from the old school of Army discipline — tough and battle-hardened.

I could see a slight glow in the corner of a wall facing towards me where my section was going.

"Get on your bellies, crows!"

I chuckled. It was Andy all right.

I gave a clear breakdown to each of my men about the ground they were covering and their arcs of fire, giving them each an area to cover with their rifles.

"If anything looks remotely suspicious let them have it" I said to Mac, "That side of the street, from that corner to that corner on the right hand, is your arc of fire. Have you made ready on the gimpy?"

"Yes" he answered.

I crawled off to my day sack and rummaged for my warm kit as the night drew in, removing my smock nervously and replacing it with the warm fleece. More shots zipped straight over my head. I threw on my webbing and squirmed across the roof tops, zig-zagging so as not to present a target. Dropping to one knee, I let a cascade of bullets flow from my rifle in the direction of the enemy muzzle flash.

The adrenaline was pumping. I got 20 rounds off and soon ran out. I dropped behind the wall and shouted 'Magazine!'

then noticed to my left and right Andy and Jono who were also blasting away along with Mac on the GPMG.

When it died down I peeked over the wall to survey the damage. As the smoke cleared, I saw a house with a nice collection of bullet holes in its walls.

"Give me a call sign, who fired that?" said the OC on the radio.

"Cpl Webster, Sir" I said, expecting a telling off.

"Good effort, keep up this aggressive stance" said the OC. "Right, don't fuck around — let's take the fight to these bastards!"

***

When the enemy fire first started pouring in, I had heard amongst the hailstorm of bullets a weapon being cocked. It had been Mac, who was manning a GPMG. Only making ready with your weapon once the enemy is firing on you is bad news, hence why I had specifically instructed him not to hesitate if he saw any threat.

"What happened there, Mac?" I asked. He was still a little flustered.

"There were two blokes with something in their hands... by the time I realised and had a chance to make ready they let rip with their AK47s... I got half a belt down at them. I know I got one before they flew down a back alley"

The lad had done okay, but really should have been ready to fire even before the situation had reached that stage. Always have one up the spout ready to go in a war zone — it's standard procedure — but he had done what so many soldiers were trained to do; not fired until fired upon. All well and good in Northern Ireland, but applying that stupid law in this bloody town centre was suicidal.

Under our rules of engagement, Mac had acted correctly. But if I had the General Purpose Machine Gun, the best killing machine in the British Army, and I saw two militia coming down the street towards me, I would have killed them without a second thought.

My opinion was this…

Tried by 12 or carried by 6.

In other words, it's better to face a jury of 12 civvies in a court hearing than be carried to the cemetery by six soldiers you never even knew.

"Remember that, all of you" I said. "Fuck the RMPs and the SIB — they're just as much the enemy as these fucks, giving us red tape to deal with under pressure"

I told Mac he'd done a good job and to keep his chin up. I didn't want one of my best blokes thinking he had done wrong. We had to keep everyone's morale up no matter what took place.

***

I crawled over to the smoking den where Jono and Andy were on their bellies, talking and getting a fag in.

"How's Mac?" Andy asked.

"Fine, did well. Got some good fire down"

"Time for a ciggy crow" he said, leaning forward and punching Jono in the arm, "bine me, red ass!"

"I hope you don't expect free fags in civvy street, Andy" was Rob's retort. We all laughed.

He calmly put the cigarette into his mouth and lit it. You could hear the crackle of the tobacco burning and the gentle glow of the embers lit up his big raggedy 'tache. Andy's big eyes twinkled in the moon light. And he smirked at me. It made me feel very safe.

But it was short-lived. The rounds started to come in thick and fast and the fags quickly went out. I turned to Jono and saw something over his shoulder moving down Baghdad Street so I moved myself quietly into the corner to get a better look. To my surprise, there were two militia men cruising up the street with AK47 assault rifles.

This was a dream come true… opportunities never usually presented themselves in such a fashion; two men armed and trying to sneak up on our position, with us having the advantage of being higher than them on the dominant ground. Plus they had street lights blinding their view of the roof, turning us into shadows.

I took up my firing position and got my body wedged into the corner. My sight picture was now running up and down on the torso of the enemy fighter…

He breathes in, breathes out, takes a half breath... then brings his weapon up toward my direction. That's my green light.

Bang bang bang bang!

He dropped like a sack of shit in my sight picture. As I glanced to the left I noticed about five of our blokes opening up on this guy and putting rounds into him. The noise was horrifically loud and the smoke from our rifles was so thick that it was hard to make out the target.

"Check firing, check firing!" Jono shouted. Silence followed and the smoke slowly thinned to reveal the dead Iraqi lying on the floor. We scanned our arcs of fire. Our line of sight was obstructed by an electric transformer generator.

Suddenly his mate opened up on us. We replied with a huge shower of gunfire, so much that the transformer started sparking and fizzing. The whole street was being ripped up with bullets. Amongst this madness there were bits of concrete and mortar hitting me in the face. It was coming from Pick, one of the most popular guys in the battalion, quiet but funny. We called him "the Prince of Iraq". At this point he was shooting in such a position that his weapon had its muzzle pointed down into the wall and the bullets were digging a hole in it.

"Pick, check firing!" I screamed, "You'll get a breech explosion and it will blow your head off you mad twat!" What he was doing was extremely dangerous, but I guess the adrenaline had taken over.

The next thing I knew the street had disappeared under pure darkness. We stopped firing and an enormous cloud of dust rose in front of us as the generator blew up and cut the power.

To my left, Browny and Jono were fighting each other. It was a surreal thing to see. The hot spent cases from Browny's rifle had apparently been flying down Jono's neck and burning his skin.

"You dick Browny, watch what you're doing!" Jono had shouted before punching him in the face.

"For fuck's sake lads! Why are we fighting each other? It's not the time!" I said.

They shook their heads and got back into the game. Tensions were running high. To anyone looking in on our behavior it would seem outrageous. But until you've been in such an intense battle situation you cannot relate to the stress reflexes you experience.

21. Gimpy

"Watch my tracer! Watch my tracer!" bellowed a confident Geordie accent from behind as we all stared intently in the enemy's direction. All of a sudden a thunderous amount of 7.62mm and tracer mixed bullets whooshed over our heads and rained down on to the enemy position.

"Left a bit, right a bit… keep it there, yes! Keep your point of fire there" screamed Lamby as Benny hit his target. "Bang on son!"

Lamby was a quiet Geordie lad but lethal in a fire fight. He was also the only lad in our multiple who had a night sight.

"He's still moving!" he shouted.

"Not for long" Benny said.

There was another burst of fire from the General Purpose Machine Gun as the bullets ripped off towards the opposite roof top, lit up by the tracer.

"He's brown bread now!" Benny told the roof.

An overwhelming feeling of joy spread through the group. It sounds macabre, but it was a huge morale boost and a great feeling when someone had a go at your platoon and ended up paying the ultimate price for it. Benny had just used a General Purpose Machine Gun, the most effective weapon in the British Army, to cut down an enemy shooter.

The GPMG was our big gun and our loyal protector but this weapon was only good with a soldier that could understand how to operate it under intense pressure. It needed lots of oil and the right gas setting and good clean ammo with no broken link. Benny was our savior, with Lamby assisting by using his night sight to guide the fire. This dynamic pair reacted like a solo unit.

It was only 3 o clock in the morning. This was going to be a long night for us to survive. We had to take the fight to the bastards to ensure we'd all be coming home as a unit the same as we'd left.

I ordered everyone to insert fresh magazines and check themselves for bullet wounds. Fortunately, there were no casualties.

"Get some water down your necks while there is a lull in the battle." said Andy.

But the 'lull' turned out to be wishful thinking, as there was another snap, snap, snap

of gunfire nearby.

I spotted the muzzle flash and pointed out where I thought the enemy's rough position was to everyone else. Then I took aim at the flickering flash of light and shot ten rounds in quick succession.

Snap, snap, snap!

This time they were closer than ever, with rounds just skimming over my head. I was reaching over the wall and pointing my rifle in the enemy's direction, blindly firing short bursts — no way was I going to stick my fat head above that wall. Hopefully my fire would keep the enemy's head down and stop him having trigger time on us. Seems I wasn't the only one with this idea — every soldier in the platoon was peeking cautiously over the wall, like a bunch of meerkats.

I would have filmed it… but some situations are just not meant to be caught on camera.

22. The Battle Heats Up

Everyone in the battalion were on their belt buckles bar one man — Trapper, the lunatic Royal Green Jacket with no helmet. Another snap, snap, snap

 — this time too close for comfort; I could feel the bullets cracking the sound barrier like a bull whip past my head. When this happened, they made a high-pitched pinging noise... Peoww, peoww! I can remember thinking they sounded just like they do in the westerns. It's not Hollywood bullshit after all — they do actually make that noise close up. But I wasn't in a Hollywood western, and the next thought to enter my head was 'these could actually kill me any second'.

"Can I have some bloody fire support now?!" I screamed.

Peoww, peoww!

"Keep this up lads, good fucking effort!"

"No retreat, no surrender!" Benny shouted in a stupid voice, momentarily raising the roof with shrieks of laughter. It was a quote from a cheesy 80's movie called The Karate Kid.

The guy trying to take me out started piping up again, and he was getting closer. Lamby was using our only night sight on another target, so we had two hopes of bagging this twat; One of them was him suddenly dropping dead of a heart attack.

The other was Trapper.

I called for him.

"Coming" he replied, almost casually. I could hear him scrabbling across the soft tar-stained roof to get into a sniper position.

The roof stank of piss because we had been there a while without the luxury of toilet breaks, but it didn't bother Trapper. He had his own night sight and was looking through it as he got himself comfortable.

"I see you" he whispered.

Snap, snap, snap!

The enemy was still firing.

And then suddenly…

Bang!

Silence.

Some of the lads applauded Trapper's handy work and the OC shouted "Well done". Trapper casually picked up his empty case and crawled off.

Another day, another corpse in his crosshairs.

***

"Listen in, cats' cocks — as you can see these chickens' dicks don't like it when they are getting killed and there is a lovely stack of dead Iraqis pilling up in the grounds of the palace — so good shooting!

"Keep an eye on your ammo. We've ordered more — whether the weasel willies at headquarters will supply us with the bullets is another matter!

"Too-da-loo, baked bean cocks!" said Big Rob.

The lads couldn't stop laughing. There was our CSM, a great big ape of a man, skipping around on the roof as if he was taking a stroll through a park on a sunny day. And it worked because it raised morale and his confidence made you feel safe.

After all, who's going to fuck with you when you've got Big Rob Warne running the show?

23. Getting The Good News

At that point the ammo arrived. There was scarcely enough for a magazine and a half.

"Come and get it," said Andy, "make it last."

"Hmmm, time for that fag I've been meaning to have... for ages. Now bine me Pickering, you fucking crow!"

Roughly translated into civvy language, that meant 'could I have a cigarette please, young Combat Recruit of Winchester Army Depot (new lad)?'

Only Andy Buller could say that and get away with it. He was an old school Colour Sergeant who everyone respected. There was another Snap, snap, snap

 followed by a swoosh

 as an RPG went straight over our heads.

"Am I ever going to get this fag?" Andy moaned.

"Did you hear those whistle blasts?" said Browny. The bastards had been using whistles to coordinate attacks from the north, south, east and west. "My knees are killing me... I need to turn around and change my position" he added. All the empty cases and bullet links were making it difficult to stay on our knees all night.

"I'll cover you" I said.

A lull in battle gives you a false sense of security. But you don't switch off. You can't switch off. The adrenaline keeps you awake anyway. Browny turned his back on the enemy and at that very second there was a whoosh

as another RPG screamed up the street and directly over his head. There was a huge boom as the warhead exploded 100 meters above the palace roof.

"Fucking hell Browny, how lucky was that!" I said.

Browny gave a nervous laugh. "That was close!" he said breathlessly.

I would like to be able to say that we located the enemy with our issued night sights and killed him... but we didn't have night sites and so the enemy ran into the night.

Another RPG hit the northern wall. The lads were in hysterics with laughter at the extreme madness surrounding us. Looking back, it was probably a combat stress reaction.

On Baghdad Street was a man lying dead in the road from earlier. A message came over the radio from Maj Pearce;

"Move down to Baghdad Street and retrieve that dead Iraqi, do it now while there is a lull in the battle."

My good friend Dave Drummond, a brilliant commander and prolific killer, led the patrol out. The call sign left the back gate. There was an eerie silence in the air, as if the militia were allowing us a break — very sporting of them indeed.

My section gave covering fire support from the roof and I watched as the call sign moved cautiously down Tigris Street and down towards Baghdad Street and near the corpse.

"Fuck me!" said Dave, "You're not going to believe this boss — he's still alive!"

"Right, pick up his weapon, don't fuck around... bring him back and we'll get the MO on him."

We watched as Dave ripped down a festival banner and used it as an improvised stretcher to get the enemy casualty back to our location. We could now hear him gargling blood as he struggled to breathe — the horrific sound of a human being trying to stay alive.

I could not say exactly what my feelings were; maybe excitement at first, then horror as the sound of a dying man made me realise how fragile we are.

As they laid the dying man on the back courtyard floor, we all peeped over to get a glimpse. His gargles were getting weaker. The OC shouted to get the MO quickly. When he arrived Rob Warne passed him some med kit and a field dressing.

"Oh my god," the MO said, "he's proper fucked!"

"You've done years at medical school to tell us he's fucked? I could have told you that" said Rob.

In the moment that the casualty took his last breath the realisation dawned on me that the man I had shot hours earlier was now dead and my life would never be the same again. I was happy but also sad and confused. I didn't know how I should feel. I never knew how to react to any of this but I had the soul of a murderer.

"Face out, stay switched on and give me that fucking bine" said Andy

"Why, are you splashing the fags Andy?"

"Am I fuck, crow!" he said as he punched me in the arm.

At the same time an RPG — and what looked like an expensive firework — came roaring up the street. It was kind of pretty, like a fiery dragon with its swirling tail dragging behind it. You want to just stand and watch, mesmerised by the display; the only problem is that this is one pyrotechnic that can seriously fuck you up. We all dived for cover.

"Utah Street, reference white car, two times enemy... watch my tracer!" said Mac as the tracer screamed down the street ripping up curbs and shredding cars. We all reacted to his clear target indication.

"Well done Mac, good one son. Did you get him?"

"Lamby what can you see on the night sight?"

"He is fucked, good and proper!" Everyone started to laugh.

"That's enough!" Andy said, "Be professional."

He was right, but it's such a weird feeling; the nerves, the excitement... it all combines and you end up relishing in the fact that some faceless stranger is going to crawl into an alley somewhere and die.

One thing didn't add up; we seemed to be using a lot of bullets for the amount of people we were killing. There are a few theories that might explain this; one is that the bullets we were using were not designed to kill in one shot. The 5.56mm bullet is designed to maim, allowing two men to drag the casualties off the battlefield three at a time. If you shot someone in the head with the 7.62mm bullets used by the old SLR, they wouldn't just make a hole in it, but take it off the target's shoulders.

Another theory is that the enemy soldiers were drugged with amphetamines in preparation to become martyrs. I had heard that some suicide bombers had secondary detonation switches for a 3rd party to initiate the bomb, just in case the bomber themselves had second thoughts.

Whatever the explanation, they were good opposition and had us fenced in.

"Enjoying the firework display, gaylords?" said Big Rob, skipping towards us on the roof. "Keep it up lads and we'll get you relieved tomorrow morning for some lovely fresh breakfast which the colour boy is risking his life to bring down."

This was welcome news as we had hardly eaten in days and water was scarce — we were worried that if the siege lasted much longer we would have to start eating the Iraqi corpses lying around.

I reached across my pocket and felt a bulge — it was my little black box. Inside was a blue beaded rosary my Nan had given to me while I was young and my mum's St Christopher that I had taken on many tours. I touched them, made a quick sign of the cross and asked for all of us to have the Lords protection so that everyone could come home alive.

Although we had been up for action from the start, we were all beginning to get tired and scared. The sky was still pitch black but to the east I could see some dark blue emerging. The conditions were poor and we needed some daylight on our side so that the Iraqis had less cover. The strip of light on the horizon was a sign of hope that we'd see this shit through till the end.

'Please don't let any of us die now, please let us all go home, please...'

 I was thinking. I kept repeating it in my head, praying to God that nothing bad would happen. I think it was at that point that I had a moment of clarity; everything in life happens for a reason, no matter how vile or amazing — you only have one life and you better make the best of it. We are all here to be tested and to learn.

"You fucking biff, stay awake!" said Head, jolting me from prayer as he emerged from his hiding place. Now that the gunfire had stopped he was up to check that his blokes weren't falling asleep. They were all petrified of him because he could be a real bully.

I turned to one of my friends.

"Well Browny, me old mucker — we're nearly at that breakfast..." There was a terrific boom in the distance. The sun was rising and it was a glorious morning. The pungent smell of stale urine and dead bodies suddenly brought me back down to earth. As I glanced nervously over the wall, I saw my mates holding their noses, such was the stench of congealed blood, and struggling to pick up the dead Iraqis piled in the courtyard of the palace. I could hear the sounds of gunfire in the distance but knew it was too far away to put my life in direct threat. The Iraqis had lost a lot of blokes the previous night and had dozens more casualties.

***

So what did my moment of clarity mean? What did I learn?

War… it's provides an adrenaline rush as powerful as any drug. After it you are physically and mentally drained. Then it all sinks in, and you have time for reflective introspection… Was I scared? Will I ever be the same?

The only thing I was sure of was that war isn't fun. Yet laughter was an integral part of our survival — had we not been able to keep spirits up with humour we may not have found the strength to keep going. It was odd, because very little of what we experienced out there would fit most people's idea of funny.

It was like when you're young and at school or a funeral, and you have a fit of the giggles… knowing you're not supposed to somehow makes you laugh even more. Fear, crying and deep belly laughs are similar physical states — they all relate to extremes of emotion. To show them in public is very powerful and infectious.

War is one big emotional roller coaster. In this situation we had to draw sides — the 'good' guys and the 'bad' guys.

It's nothing personal, that's just the way it is to survive. We weren't journalists. We certainly weren't politicians. We were soldiers being paid to wreak havoc and fuck people up with dangerous weapons.

If you're going to join the Army this century then expect to be called upon to kill and maim people. Every bit of training we did was geared towards making us killers. If you join for any other reason then you're simply in the wrong job.

War is madness... to survive madness you must become madness. And fight like a bastard.

The rest is up to luck and fate but your soul will never be the same again once you cross that line.

24. The Enemy

The Mahdi Army was a formidable opponent. Despite Saddam Hussein's reign of tyranny he was never able to dominate the marshland tribes of Maysan Province or the Shia-dominant population of the city of Amarah. The British Army had little chance of dominating the area with less than 300 men.

We had descaled our company of men by handing in vital kit during the last week before passing it over to the PWRR, who at this point had been told that the situation was calming down and that they could expect a quiet tour. As a result, they were not prepared for what lay ahead that summer.

It wasn't their fault; they were going by the intelligence that had been gathered and fed to their head shed. However they were going to a warzone, not a dinner party, and they should have been ready for every eventuality including the worst. That way, when the shit hit the fan they would have at least had real weapons rather than the drill barrels that their inexperienced mortar platoon turned up with. They thought it would be so quiet that they could conduct training in Iraq for promotional courses and so forth. I believe 81mm mortar is essential small compact artillery and should always be accessible to infantry. But on this occasion, we had to sign ours over to them.

Sadly, many lives were lost and some of them were honoured posthumously with awards including the Victoria Cross and Military Cross, plus countless mentions in dispatches. I take my hat off to them — it was a shitty situation they were in and they did well.

***

The Iraqi soldiers we were coming across were brave bastards, probably fighting for money to provide for their family. But they were still the enemy, so when the opportunity arose to send one of them to heaven on 'Flight 5.56mm', we as soldiers had no alternative. It had been announced on the BBC World Service that the Italian soldiers had fled and given up their palace further down the line. So considering the odds against us, we were making real waves against the Mahdi Army in the town centre.

Saddam ruled Iraq with a great big clunking iron fist which he would use to crush his opponents immediately. I was starting to see why democracy didn't stand a chance here. Perhaps it could happen one day when their civilisation had moved forward, but at that time they were not ready for it. Besides which, who were we to tell these people how to live in the first place?

Our mission right now was to survive enough days and get home in one piece. So far it was going well; we had killed many of them without losing any of ours.

Muqtada al-Sadr was a big opposer of the west and the coalition. He was 30 years of age and full of fire, seen by Muslim chiefs at the time as a charismatic young radical. He had earned a devoted following, having renamed the ghettos of Baghdad as 'Sadr City' in memory of his father who was murdered by Saddam in 1999. He was not the type to bow down to pressure from the US or British government. One headline in The Sun newspaper in 2003 read 'Crisis in Iraq! Gun battles escalate'

. We had a huge fight on our hands.

Sadr controlled a militia of several thousand who wanted to see him as the country's leader. They were opposed by the coalition. Because of this Sadr called for his followers to terrorise their enemies when the infrastructure promised by the coalition was not delivered. We were perceived as occupiers of their land. More grim headlines were making the papers back home; 'Brits hurt — six British soldiers were injured fighting and 15 Iraqis were killed in gun battles yesterday across the country'

 was one such quote from The Sun.

The clash in Amarah was one of several between coalition forces and heavily armed militia loyal to al-Sadr. With violence reported in all major cities, British commanders grew concerned for the 11,000 strong force facing attacks. The Ministry Of Defence said: 'We are aware that 15 Iraqis have been killed in Amarah and six soldiers have been injured, none seriously. In Nasiriyah 500 Italian troops under British command fought a fierce dawn battle with the militia killing 15 and wounding 35. 12 Italians were injured.'

That was some of the back page bullshit the media were being fed by the MOD press office. It was just filtered spin, as usual, as the government tried hard to keep all of the chaos under wraps.

25. Glorious Morning

The sun was up and shining more radiantly than ever. It had never felt this good to see morning.

After a night of intense fighting, everyone was too drained to talk. We were all sporting the same vacant gaze. I knew that we would never forget the previous night, and having been through it together we now had a common bond. All the petty squabbling that I got so uptight about seemed stupid. These men had helped me to survive — they were my friends.

"I'm starving." Browny said quietly.

"That's a shock, fat boy" Jono said mockingly. "Sorry about hitting you last night — I lost it"

"That's okay. Let's go and get fed" said Browny, pushing everyone out of the way to get to the front of the food queue.

Liam turned to me and said, "I told you you'd shit yourself when bullets are flying over your head!"

"Okay mate," I replied, zombie-like, "you're totally right, I'll never pray for it again. Last night was scary and I got the lesson I deserved."

Liam burst out laughing. After the invasion he had been involved with, I hassled him all the time to find out what it was like to be in an extreme battle. I wasn't sure I believed him when he told me it was shit-your-pants scary. But he was right; ask any honest soldier how they react to warfare and they'll tell you the same, even if they enjoyed parts of it. No matter how much of a warrior you consider yourself, it is human nature to feel fear when your life is under threat.

As we got our breakfast, the CO and RSM dished out the sausages and bacon. An Army breakfast had never tasted that good before. I shoveled it in while Liam sat smugly in front of me with his arms crossed.

"Told you, see?" he said, "but you wouldn't listen to me."

I just ignored him. I was enjoying the food too much.

"Right lads; we've got about an hour then will be on reserve back over at the palace for public order... so kit on in figures 10" said Jono.

The lack of sleep was now taking its toll. We all kitted up and dragged our exhausted bodies back over to the palace where Milan Platoon guarded the roof top. They had fired so many rounds the previous night that there was no space left to kneel. Head was in charge as his

bad knees prevented him from being on the ground that day with his own team. Rob Warne volunteered his services in his place.

We decided to try and get twenty minutes rest in the courtyard, but our deep sleep was disturbed by the noise of exploding bombs as the political situation blared from the radio.

26. Crossing The Line

After 25 minutes of broken sleep, there was an earth-shuddering boom. We awoke to hear screaming coming from the back gate. We picked up our shields and moved to the entrance of the palace before another explosion went off nearby.

"Fucking bastards!" a soldier screamed. We looked to our left and Buey was on the ground, clutching his feet in agony.

"Medic!" shouted Womble as he came running down to us. He was frantically asking for field dressing because Buey's toes had been blown off.

Buey was so big that we nicknamed him 'Bue-bacca' after Chewbacca from Star Wars. Poor guy; he was a TA lad, totally harmless and now toeless.

We could hear the Iraqi kids' laughter coming over the wall. This time their grenade had claimed a victim and they were buzzing, just the same as our soldiers had been when we inflicted pain and misery on our enemies. It was time for us to be more aggressive.

We ran out to the street. This time Rob Warne had his men ready to put plastic bullets down straight away. The previous day we had fired 180 plastic rounds, in contrast to Drumcree in Northern Ireland where we went through a week of hell but fired none due to intense media scrutiny. We were doing well but needed to keep up the hard stance so that they knew we meant business.

The mentally ill man from the day before was once again sent towards us by the crowd. As he got closer we saw that he was carrying a grenade, but couldn't see whether or not the pin was in. We squirmed uneasily as he approached, not knowing how much of a threat he posed — for all we knew he was wired with explosives.

"Arrest him, Webby" Maj Pearce ordered.

I pulled a cigarette from my pocket and leant forward through the shields. As he came closer and took it from my hand I grabbed his sleeve and pulled him violently towards me. His other arm flailed as he struggled and the grenade dropped to the floor directly in front of us.

"The pin is in!" Big Al shouted. But my pin had been pulled when the assailant resisted arrest.

I drove my elbow into his cheekbone and felt it crack. He screamed in agony as he fell to the ground and started kicking up at me. I drew my weapon and put it to his face and cocked it

as a challenge. He was trying to grab my weapon so I pushed the barrel against him and pinned him to the floor with the muzzle.

"You will die, do you want to fucking die?!" I screamed at the top of my lungs.

"Webby! Calm down and let Big Al take him off your hands" said Maj Pearce. He was a man I had great respect for, and his was quite possibly the only voice that could have gotten through to me at that point. I broke from my fit of rage when I heard his order.

"Sorry sir" I replied.

"Move back up to the roof and cool off." Maj Pearce said calmly.

I looked up and the crowd of rioters had moved back. Some of them looked shocked by my behavior. So was I.

I was losing my sense of compassion and believe I had crossed a point of no return. On reflection I believe that these were the early symptoms of Post-Traumatic Stress Disorder.

27. A Roof with a View

I went back up to the roof as Maj Pearce had instructed and decided that I would observe the rest of the rioting. As I looked down I noticed that the soldiers had changed tactics — they had dropped their shields and pulled back into the confines of the palace. I had no idea what was going on. Information came over the radio that Maj Pearce and his team had moved over to CIMIC-House to get orders from Maj Proctor. I hadn't seen Proctor about for days, which was strange because he was the commander of that area.

It was at this point that an onslaught of grenades came into the compound. They were flaring up, taking advantage of the lack of soldiers on the streets.

We had been told on the roof that we were allowed to use our own cameras to film so that it could be used as video evidence in court. I decided to take mine out and start filming.

Rob Warne, still in charge of Head's team, moved into position. I watched his mad plan unfold through my camera lens.

"Go, go, go!" he cried. They flew out of the gate, nine men running at full pelt towards the rioters.

I captured the incident in its entirety — they grabbed a handful of the worst offenders and dragged them towards the compound. My heart started pounding with excitement because I knew that the lads were about to dish out some rough justice.

I was giddily screaming profanities and egging the soldiers on, even though they couldn't hear me. I cared nothing for the kids they had captured — moments before they had been throwing explosives trying to injure or kill my friends. I became frenzied and wanted to join in. As I turned to run to the stairs I dropped my camera on the floor. When I picked it up again it had stopped working. I was so devastated at the thought of losing that footage that by the time I got downstairs the beating had finished and they had been taken to the Iraqi Police.

***

Later I watched the footage back. I didn't think for a moment that it would have any impact. This sort of violence, and much worse, was around us all the time. In relative terms to our circumstances, it was normal. 24 hours previous I had killed a man. Now I was behaving like an animal. There was no going back. I could either stop and try to forgive myself for the violence and pain I had unleashed, or keep killing until I was numb.

Later that night I spoke to Womble about the incident. He was very angry at the kids who had been constantly throwing grenades over the course of three days. He felt the kicking was justified. At the time so did I.

28. Battle Fatigue

That afternoon I was starting to get an itchy trigger finger stood on the roof so volunteered my services for a night patrol.

"You sure? It's only a private's job you'll be doing and it's a dodgy foot patrol over the Tigris with Milan Platoon"

But I was keen as ever to make the most of this experience while it lasted.

Leading the mission was Captain Burns, who shook my hand and told me I would be rear man on Cpl Riggs's section. He gave us the brief;

"The intelligence is that many small groups of militia are out there trying to take our supply vehicle routes out, so we're going out to show presence and dominate the ground. The Colonel is adamant that you all understand that this is a reconnaissance patrol, not a fighting patrol — am I clear?"

"Yes Sir" we replied in unison.

A recce patrol is classed as defensive operations, and a fighting patrol is classed as offensive operations. The CO had overheard two soldiers bragging about how they had been out hunting the enemy on a fighting patrol. Given that the war was considered to be ending and the government was trying to keep a lid on things in Iraq, mention of a new war brewing would be a disaster. Captain Burns's tone of voice suggested that things were not going at all well in Westminster.

As we prepared to deploy our patrol, I heard a massive explosion outside. RPGs were already being launched at us under the cover of darkness. We assembled in the forecourt to do last minute kit checks. I met up with Cocky, the second to last man on the patrol. We performed some safety checks for each other.

"You watch my ass and I'll watch yours" he said.

I saw Mitch coming in from the last patrol. He looked worn out — they had been involved in some intense fighting by the looks of it.

"Fuck me, it's crazy out there! We shot and killed three Iraqis. They had set an ambush up for our supply vehicles and as we came around the corner they were there waiting but didn't notice us. So we formed an extended line and set up a snap ambush. We whispered on our

radio 'after three, let them have it'… then shot fuck out of them, searched them and left them on the side of the road" I was starting to tingle with excitement for this patrol.

I headed up to the near gate and waited just inside as Cpl Riggs, the Commander, gave us the countdown. There was a 200 metre stretch to cover before we were clear of camp, which is where the enemy snipers would concentrate their gunfire. Our plan was simple; run for our lives.

"Go, go, go!" roared the corporal. We went one by one, leaving a ten metre gap between each man to give the enemy a smaller target to hit. I was the last one to go and, as I listened for gunfire, it dawned on me that the point man and the last man were the most vulnerable targets. My heart was in my throat, but I was also excited for a leg stretch.

Before I knew it I was the only one left. Out I ran, down Tigris Street until I had cleared the main drag and could jump left down to Baghdad Street.

"Last man out!" I sent down the radio to Riggs.

You could hear a pin drop... there was not a soul in sight. No sound from a radio or TV, no children playing — just eerie silence. And it was so early. We used the term 'combat indicator' to describe the gut feeling we experienced when something was amiss. I was starting to get that gut feeling.

It turned out that there had been a curfew imposed by the Iraqi police. It was a case of not if, but when were we going to 'get the good news' as we tip-toed quietly through the streets.

As I neared the end of Baghdad Street I could see blood stains on the floor where the guy I'd shot the previous night had lay dying. I looked up to where I fired from. The power was back on now, but I could see nothing on the palace roof top. Even though his weapon had been pointing at me and my friends, there's no way he would have been able to see us — the lights were too blinding.

As we moved through the streets I heard a radio coming from an open market shop. I poked my head around and waved at the man using it.

"As-salaamu alaikum" I said quietly.

He said "Wa alaikum as-salaam" and we looked at each other. Even though we didn't speak the same language, I could tell that we were thinking similar things. We're all human beings at the end of the day. Two men just trying to make a living. Yet we were both sneaking around in this fucked-up kill-zone and neither of us could even explain why.

We nodded to one another and he said something in Arabic. I understood the implication and replied "I know mate".

***

We could hear gunfire coming from the northern end of the city. Riggs decided to move us out towards the Tigris riverbank to escape the exposing street lamps.

We had to sprint across the main road again in case of snipers. Once under the river's main bridge, we had to do a quick check for IEDs and command wires — anything that could blow the bridge during tomorrow's antics.

Our silhouettes stretched high across the ground as we patrolled the bridge. I got very bored being the end man, so decided to lighten the situation with a bit of childish humour.

"Cocky" I whispered as I drew my pants down past my knees, tucked my dick between my legs and did the 'Bangkok ladyboy dance' over the River Tigris. Cocky was in hysterics and called me a 'fucking idiot' but it got a cheap laugh. And yes, I was a Corporal and yes, I should have known better. But soldier humour can be pretty close to the bone, so to speak.

We patrolled past the Sadr building and tried to quickly nick some of his banners and posters to keep as memorabilia, but they were too well pasted on. We ducked in and out of the shadows to the north of the palace and then through a very poor part of Amarah where many of the buildings were made of wicker straw and Mud. The local hounds were barking like mad, giving our location away and as we passed some tall palm trees we were suddenly lit up by 81mm mortar illume rounds. Everyone dropped to the ground and stayed still as possible.

No one was aware at the time that part of my platoon had been sent back to camp Abu Naji to provide fire support weapons. The militia seemed to have realised they weren't going to penetrate CIMIC-House and take over the Pink Palace, so had concentrated their efforts back on our main camp where all the top brass were controlling the operation. They had caught us with our pants down as all of our troops were in the town centre, which explained why we saw very little action on our patrol.

Once the illume firework display had ended we quickly made our way back to the safety of the palace. It was now about four in the morning and I'd had hardly any sleep in four days, so was running purely on adrenaline. Maj Pearce and Rob Warne were stood by a Land Rover discussing the daylight tactics.

"They're taking a right pounding in Abu Naji tonight and have no soldiers" Big Rob told me, "they've got the chefs manning the sangars and guard room on the camp. They're in shit state."

The radio was chock-a-block with call signs under fire around the city, but the palace seemed relatively quiet and the Sadr Mahdi Army were testing our nerve by hitting Abu Naji hard.

"Webby, go and get your head down son," Maj Pearce told me, calm as ever, "we've got a long day ahead."

29. Just Another Day At War

I only had about an hour's kip that night — there was a mortar attack at 5am which made me really jumpy. When I got up I felt delirious.

At breakfast over at CIMIC-House Maj Pearce had a plan; he wanted to send the main Medical Officer to Camp Abu Naji.

"Webster and Womble will escort the MO. Webby, you can work back with the mortar platoon in camp." said the OC.

I was a spare Corporal and the town had quietened down, so this decision made sense. I was gutted to be going back but since the Mahdi Army seemed to be aiming their fire at Abu Naji I thought it may have been a blessing. Plus there was a chance I'd get to fire live mortars.

I now realise Maj James Pearce was making a decision to send me and Womble back based on our behaviour as we were showing clear signs of battle fatigue. We needed to cool down after the incident the day before with the arrest I made. This was a very good command decision. Pearce never made you feel like you were a failure or that you couldn't handle the pressure.

Despite this, his leadership would later be unfairly brought into question by his superiors.

***

After returning in a non-armoured Land Rover with no escort (a potentially suicidal move during the daytime) we arrived back at camp to find the lads sunbathing. I needed to get some sleep as we were on standby all night to man the mortar barrels. There was a lot of animosity amongst the men who were sent back early and not in the thick of it in town with the rest of the company.

I managed to get some sleep for the first time in four days. Cpl Bridges was in charge and I told him that I would like to be No.1 on the mortar that would be firing rather than sat back controlling the mortar line.

30. Incoming

We had noticed that the arriving PWRR didn't seem particularly confident or proactive. They were parking up lots of Saxon vehicles, which had been fantastic in Northern Ireland. How effective they would be in Iraq was for them to find out.

I also questioned why there was no ECM. These are used to combat IEDs and have been around for decades in the British Army. In Northern Ireland it would have been considered madness to leave base without them. On this day one of our vehicles was blown up — had it been carrying ECM it would not have been hit. Any soldier who has used this equipment knows how effective they are in preventing explosions, yet we didn't have any in Iraq.

Our mortar line was set up on the football pitch — three mortar barrels mounted in the back of 1950's style FV432 armoured fighting vehicles. In other words, heaps of shit, but it was the only effective mortar cover on the whole camp so providing there were no direct hits they were in a safe place.

We had laid all the relevant target information onto our sights and were waiting for night fall. Whatty was my No.2. It was tight for space in the tanks and with all the ammo behind me I could barely move. On the radio was Shelly, the oldest corporal I had ever known... I used to say he probably joined and fought in the Napoleonic wars.

Whatty had a mini DVD player and we had a pirate copy of "Lord of the Rings" to watch, so we got into our sleeping bags ready for a cosy night inside a vehicle designed to kill and maim. Rather ironic I thought.

Halfway through the film there were some incredible sound effects which weren't coming from the DVD player; a high pitched shriek followed by a boom, then the tink, tink, tink

 of shrapnel blasting against the sides of the tank.

"Incoming!" someone shouted.

'No shit

,' I thought, 'where the fuck's my helmet!?' There were further booms as three more strikes landed in quick succession around our vehicle.

"What's the score, Shelly?" I enquired.

"Reconnaissance Platoon have located the firing point from these mortars and have told us to lay on to target X13" Shelly shouted back.

We had these coordinates already written — it just came down now to how fast we could apply the information to the mortar sights and get them on target to kill the enemy.

Whatty was drawing out a high explosive mortar round and standing to my left with his finger through the pin which arms the bomb. He was waiting for my order to put it down the barrel — in 30 seconds the enemy should have been feeling large slivers of white hot metal puncturing vital organs.

"On!" I shouted anxiously.

"Check firing! Check firing!" Shelly interrupted, "Do not fire, we've been told not to fire until we have contacted Whitehall in London."

"What?!" We were under attack — why did the government back home in England get to make that call? "Fuck them, the white collar twats!" I yelled to Shelly.

Whatty shook his head, taking his finger out of the safety pin and putting the bomb back in the rack.

"Fucking stuck up pricks," he said, seething with anger, "I'd love for them to come out here and take this shit."

Five minutes went by and Whitehall still had not given us the green light. By this point we could have neutralised the target and prevented further attacks on the base.

When ten minutes had elapsed, Shelly shouted out "X11 illumination fuse setting 30 at my command, 10 rounds fire for effect."

I didn't have time to moan at that pathetic order given by some weak bastard in London.

As the rounds went down I had to listen to the radio, yet the new headsets did not allow for the mortar ear defence. As each bomb went off, it felt like there were hot knitting needles being rammed into my earholes.

"Last round!" shouted Whatty.

"What the fuck was that all about Shelly, what are they playing at?" I asked. Shelly went silent as he listened to the main radio net.

"Recce Platoon have said the enemy have packed up and gone, but thanks for the illume… it looked really nice" said Shelly sarcastically.

Who did they think they were telling us what to do in military situations? We could and should have wiped out the threat from this highly motivated, highly accurate enemy mortar unit. Whitehall's excuse was that the enemy was a mile from a small village. They didn't want to risk

the collateral damage. I never understood how a pen-pushing white collar was allowed control over whether I lived or died in a combat zone to save a diplomatic incident.

That was the last of the incoming we received that night. We had a couple of illumination fire missions but got to watch the end of "Lord of the Rings".

31. Handing Over

After a patchy night's sleep we woke and went to check out the craters left by the incoming mortars. All of them were very close to our mortar line on the football pitch and only an enemy with inside information on key targets could have hit with such precision. As if to confirm this theory, the tent where three locals washed our dishes was completely destroyed. One of our fridges was completely peppered in shrapnel holes. Our pot washers had obviously been working not only for us, but also for the enemy.

That day we were supposed to hand over the mortar line to the incoming PWRR but there was a big problem; the regiment had brought none of their own barrels, only APL's, implying that they thought it would be quiet enough for them to polish their skills.

Bridgey came to the mortar line to brief us up.

"Right lads," he said, "we need to stay here tonight and will hand over to the PWRR tomorrow. I'm taking their Mortar Platoon Commander through all of the targets and drills tonight."

After another night of madness the town had gone quiet again. I even thought they were giving us a break so we could hand over the keys to hell. The company had returned to Abu Naji and all we had to do was pack up and go. Everyone was handing in their riot kit along with their moducts and specialist equipment.

The PWRR were now manning the mortar line with one barrel instead of three, which would be no protection for a camp this size. They had no armoured vehicles and had dug a mortar trench. It felt like we were handing over a giant hornet's nest that we had whacked with a big stick before pissing off.

But maybe we weren't leaving just yet… Rob Warne told me that the Americans were going into Fallujah and we may have been needed to back them up.

"They can't do that! How much longer will we have to stay out here?" I said.

"Four months mate. I'm going on a meeting at 1100 — I'll brief the company then." Rob answered.

Talk about moving the goal posts at the last minute. I had had enough now and so had the lads. They were demoralised by this news but we could do nothing but wait until 11am.

32. The Late Flight Home

"Carry on packing," said Rob as he returned from his meeting, "they are putting the attack off so we are in the clear!"

The relief was felt all over the company; we were out of there that afternoon. The list of flights was produced and I was on Flight 3. I wondered what crazy plan they had devised to get a whole battalion out of here.

For our last night we managed to get some beers and have a secret party at the back of our tent. We had about four cans each and were shit-faced. Keo couldn't stand and pissed all over himself. We all laughed and discussed what we achieved in the time we had spent there.

"I was involved in the invasion and between my arrival and departure we had achieved nothing" said Liam. Harrison, who had just come out of the hospital after being shot in the ass, agreed. We all went to bed and the mortar fire started again at about midnight. Norwegian engineers had built mortar-proof accommodation for us but it was 500 metres away and it was a bigger risk to run to the protective building than it was to just lie in the tent and pray to God.

***

That morning the mood was good. We mounted the bus and watched the new regiment getting to grips with their new home. They started to frantically mount their Saxon wagons and head out the front gate. As we left through the back gate, we were all giving them the 'V's' and wanker signs. It was an old tradition; shouting 'stag on losers' and singing 'we're all going on a summer holiday' — basically really rubbing it in that our tour of hell had ended while theirs was just beginning.

As we headed towards Sparrow Hark Airport, we looked back from our rickety old bus and could see burning black smoke in the town centre. It was the Saxons — the locals were giving the PWRR their baptism of fire. The Warriors that were escorting us to freedom abruptly broke off and drove towards the town and we realised that the bus was turning around to head back to the gate and the men that we had just been shouting profanities at. You could see the look of delight on their faces.

As we got off the bus with no ammo and all our kit in our hands we could hear gunfire and explosions. We sat in camp for another hour before getting the message that we were leaving.

"Please hurry up" Browny shouted. The rest of us looked up to the sky and saw an aircraft approaching. As it landed and screeched to a halt the RSM came running out and said;

"No pissing around, let's go!"

We ran in two lines onto the loading bay at the rear of the Hercules, bags in the middle, seatbelts on. We all looked apprehensive as they got the last man on. I was sat next to the RSM.

I could still hear gunfire outside as the plane roared to life and began to pick up speed.

"Come on you bastard, let's go!" Browny yelled.

The wheels left the ground and we were airborne. I could see through the back of the tailgate gunner that we were flying low to put off RPG attacks. Chaff was being blown to throw off heat seeking surface-to-air missiles.

"Well Cpl Webster," the RSM said, "we made it!"

We were leaving hell behind.

Or so I thought.

33. Welcome Home

We were all relaxing on the flight home from Basra and thinking about what we had witnessed over the last few days. I started to think of those we had left behind, such as 'Fingers'. I wondered how his family would be coping. I thought of Maj Turner, our battalion 2IC who had lost family in a car accident in Germany while he was serving in Iraq. I wondered how he was coming to terms with his loss.

I thought of Asad, our Iraqi interpreter, and hoped he would be looked after as he was a true gentleman who kept us alive on many patrols. And finally I thought about the people we had killed out there. Was Iraq a better place because of it?

It was a quiet night as we touched down at Hanover Airport where we were bundled straight onto the coaches. Everyone was tired and had had enough of each other. I was looking forward to get back to my own room and have my own space and do what the hell I wanted. Married men were excited about seeing their kids... there were lots of newborns so for some it would be the first time. But us single lads just couldn't wait to have leave and enjoy our lives again. For me and Liam that meant getting out to our properties in Spain.

As we entered the camp we noticed converse signs on either side of the street — one was an anti-war banner which read 'BABYKILLERS', the other was a big sign on the camp gates with the words 'WELCOME HOME LADS'.

It was a lovely feeling to be back and as we pulled onto the main square the coaches were surrounded by excited sons and daughters and happy wives.

As we came off the bus we were greeted by Steve Mort, the families' officer, and we moved into the gym for a can of beer and some welcome back speeches and rules. The gym had been decorated by the kids with colourful banners and drawings. Liam and I felt quite empty as, although we had nice properties in Spain and money in the bank, we had no one to miss us while we were away. If we had been killed would it have really mattered with no dependants?

To cheer Liam up I said, "Shall I run up to the punch bags and scream 'I'm crazy because of the war' and start smacking ten barrels of shit out of them?" He laughed at what would turn out to be a strangely prophetic comment.

We listened to the speech from Maj Noble, the acting CO.

"It's 3am. Single lads, have your beers and go back to your rooms; you are all confined to camp for 24 hours. Get some sleep and sort your rooms out. Next parade is in a day's time." He told us.

It seemed that they had laid on a fantastic welcome home for married personnel, who could go out with their families and enjoy the world as civilised human beings. I felt that we were being treated like animals as we headed off to our rooms, away from the sound of cheering and laughter in the gym.

34. Thief In The Barracks

The first thing I noticed when I got back to my room was that my entire DVD collection was missing. I jumped to the conclusion that I had been robbed, so went outside to look for signs of forced entry. At that point, I saw Whatty and Smudge coming down the corridor towards me. They looked angry.

"Our rooms have been used, our beds have been moved around and slept in, there's rubbish in the bins and our computer games have been stolen" fumed Whatty.

We had to log what was missing and report it to the Colour Sergeant in charge of accommodation. Pick said that his DVDs had also been taken. There were quite a few whose rooms were not as they had left them yet there were no signs of forced entry. I was furious. But it wouldn't take long to catch the thief, as he hadn't covered his tracks very well; Whatty found a game in his PlayStation labelled with the suspected culprit's name.

Rfn Hendricks was a Green Jacket who was too sick to go out to Iraq so was appointed as our block holder while we were away. He was trusted with the keys to all rooms and looked after our car keys.

"Where the fuck is Rifleman Hendricks?" I seethed. I was looking for blood and not thinking straight — had he walked in at that moment I could have possibly beaten him to death.

I found one of my DVDs in another block. When I asked the person using it who had given it to him, he told me it was Hendricks. That was all the evidence I needed.

I went to the Colour Sergeant who told me to report it to the RMP, which I did. I explained to the guy on the end of the phone how much stuff Hendricks had nicked, but he wasn't interested because the rooms had not been broken into. So I told the monkey bastard we would sort it out ourselves and slammed the phone down.

The next morning we found more incriminating evidence, this time particularly sickening; Hendricks had been driving our dead friend Fingers' car because he knew he wasn't coming home.

That was the last straw; he was going down.

***

I was on duty the next day. The company was on parade and when I walked out to take their register Rfn Hendricks was there stood looking at me as if nothing had happened.

"Right gents," I said calmly, "before I take this register I want to see a show of hands — who has had kit stolen from their rooms?" Lots of hands went up. From my pocket I pulled out my DVD and held it in front of Hendricks' face. I asked him how it had disappeared from my room and ended up in another block — one that he had the keys to.

"I don't know mate" Hendricks said, gulping with guilt.

"And why the fuck have you been driving Fingers' car?!" I bellowed. I didn't let him answer; with the anger I had pouring out I crushed the DVD in my hand and swiftly drove it into his throat before violently pushing him to the floor.

"Stealing from dead people and nicking our kit while in Iraq!" I screamed at him. The company froze — everyone seemed scared but no one said anything. I had become a very violent individual with the ability to kill any human being if I believed it was the right thing to do. We all had the potential to be extremely dangerous and were about to be released into society.

I walked off to calm down and when I got to my room I put the battered discs in a towel and sat on them. Five minutes later Rob Warne came to my door so I told him what had just happened and why. He said "Good — well done" but warned me I should sort out my story as the military police were on their way to arrest me.

"Oh, now they want to know" I muttered, hearing them walk down the corridor.

"Corporal Webster," said one as they reached my door, "I'm arresting you for the assault of Rifleman Hendricks"

Two days later Hendricks dropped the charges as he had no witnesses. Funny thing — even though the whole company had been there when it happened, apparently nobody had seen it.

Nobody, that is, who wasn't too afraid of me to come forward.

35. Embarkation Leave

After a couple of weeks in camp we had to arrange our post-tour embarkation leave. Liam and I were all booked up to fly out to Spain where we planned to relax.

When we arrived at Alicante Airport we started to wonder if we had made the right decision coming out to another hot country. We had already endured six months of intense heat in Iraq and the last thing we wanted was to be surrounded by conditions that reminded us of that place. Even at this point I think the anticlimax of civilian life was starting to kick in following the intense adrenaline rush of war. Liam was feeling more of the effects as he had spent nearly ten months in conflict and with only a handful of months between tours no one knew what was going on in his mind.

My flat in the town centre was rented out to some Moroccans, so we stayed at his house with his parents. As always they were very accommodating. After a couple of days we showed them the footage I had shot out in Iraq. They were quite shocked at the level of violence we had been subjected to. They warned me to be careful about who I showed the video.

I found this hard to understand — we thought it was pretty normal. This is how war is... why would it offend anyone? Why should we hide it from the public eye? We were sent to war by our country, this is what we faced and this is how we dealt with those situations.

Liam didn't let it bother him so much but it really frustrated me as no one seemed to care for what we had done.

***

The next day all of the expats were rushing to buy a copy of the Spanish Mirror. The headline was 'Outrage!' with the picture of a supposed Iraqi detainee with a sandbag over his head and being pissed on by a supposed British soldier.

My initial reaction, even as a soldier, was to believe it. But as me and Liam studied the photo more carefully we noticed some things that did not add up. Firstly, the 'prisoner' was wearing a t-shirt with the Iraqi flag on it, and I had never once seen an Iraqi proud enough of his fallen country to wear such a garment. Secondly, it looked more like the 'soldier' was squirting water from a bottle than urinating. Thirdly, he was stood on an army Bedford 4 ton vehicle, which is probably not what they would have been using. The whole thing stank.

The media was having a field day over the alleged behaviour. This was the last thing the PWRR needed as they were already having a terrible tour of duty and now they had to answer to this.

We felt so depressed that the media would not let it go. Every soldier was suddenly in the firing line. One minute it was 'our boys', the next it was 'scum, bullies, animals'.

Sometimes I really wonder if people understand what a soldier's job entails. You would think the media would get behind British Forces. It seemed they only did that when one or some of us were killed.

I suggested to Liam we go up north and stay in a hotel to lift our spirits because this holiday was turning into a disaster. We headed to a famous golf course where some Birmingham City fans had been involved in a rape scandal three weeks previous.

On the way we stopped off at a karaoke night and were chatting up the bar staff in the English theme pub. As soon as we told the girls we were soldiers it was like alarm bells had gone off in their heads. They brought up the abuse pictures and one of the girls warned us to keep our occupations to ourselves as the male bar worker was a Moroccan al-Qaeda supporter and training to go to Afghanistan to fight British and American troops.

Liam pushed his pint away and walked outside unhappily. I suggested that we continue to the golf course and not mention what we did, who we were, or where we came from to anyone. The word Iraq was banned.

"Deal!" Liam said, and we headed for the green.

We soon realised why it was football players that drank there — each round cost around ten Euros. However, we did meet two women who were married to aircraft pilots in the RAF. When they asked what we did we said "we screw the caps onto tooth paste tubes." They seemed to find us amusing and it turned the night around so we ended up getting shit-faced.

On the walk home one of the RAF wives asked where we were staying. Trying to keep a straight face we explained it

141

was only two minutes up the road. They were probably expecting a luxury apartment.

"Here we are ladies, the Hotel Paradiso!" said Liam pointing at his loan silver Ford Focus, covered in dust with no tax and uninsured. They burst out laughing thinking we were pulling their legs.

"Night ladies" I said, opening the boot and pulling out two Army issue sleeping bags. I flipped a coin and told Liam to call heads or tails. Unluckily for him he lost the toss and got the steering wheel and brakes side. We got into the car quite pleased with ourselves for getting drunk and having a laugh on 50 Euros.

Neither of us could wait to go home. Spain was good for a holiday but there was no place in the world I would rather be than Cornwall. I flew home to England leaving Spain behind and knew I had made a big mistake buying a property there.

As soon as I got to the UK I got on a train and headed westward. Even now if I cross the river over the Tamar Bridge I get goose bumps and a warm feeling. It's the Cornishman in me.

***

Liam's dad had rustled up a surprise 'welcome home from Iraq' party and invited some old friends and family. It was a beautiful sunny day in Falmouth and we got hammered at a local bar with Liam's two older brothers Jason and Shawn. I got on with Jason really well because we had similar personalities. He was one of the funniest people I had ever served with and a true friend.

That afternoon a girl I had gone to school with walked into the bar and was looking very well indeed. I hadn't seen her in a long time but we hit it off immediately.

It wasn't long before we were dating but my being in the Army made things tricky. Most women don't want their man going off to do their job in some far away land, let alone fighting wars.

Liam had also started a relationship and was all loved up. We both knew the road back to Germany would be difficult.

36. Gulf War Syndrome

The 15 hour drive from Falmouth to Paderborn on the Sunday morning was the drive from hell. We were both paying a heavy price for getting so pissed over leave — Liam was behind the wheel and detoxing so badly that when we stopped for a break he couldn't stop his hands from shaking. We were relieved to get home safely.

There wasn't really much on back at the barracks. We were just keeping our fitness levels up and doing pointless military tasks. Jason, Liam's brother, was going back out to Iraq. He was in charge of the battalion bar so left us to run it. A lot had changed… people were acting differently after leave and many soldiers had signed off.

I needed a bit of spare cash and decided to make a film by gathering all of the videos and DVDs other soldiers had from Iraq and editing them together. My problem was that I didn't know how to use computers, but my friend Baxter did. I'd known him for seven years during which time we'd made dozens of amateur comedy shorts together. He wasn't flavour of the month with the 'head shed' as he had an injury which meant he could not come on Op Telic 3 with the rest of us.

I had a bag of about nine tapes all together, three of which were mine. I got Baxter to take them home and see if he could download them on to his PC. He said he would so that we could work on it together over the weekend.

The next day Baxter knocked at my door and told me he couldn't download it onto his computer hard drive. I had no reason not to believe him as we had been very good mates for a long time.

That afternoon I went through the tapes to find the best scenes for my documentary. As I did it dawned on me that some of the material could get soldiers into a lot of trouble, including the beating scene I had filmed from the roof. The more I watched the more it started to feel like we had all taken part in a movie — never before had the military allowed soldiers on the front line to film war in its entirety. Some scenes were quite graphic and would almost certainly cause outrage to the public. Looking back it's easy to see that I should have been more cautious.

However due to my naivety (and a degree of pure stupidity) I approached Matty Lavers to help produce and edit a documentary for me.

We set up a miniature studio in his room and went through the scenes, although we didn't have time to scrutinise every last one of them.

We added a sound track using artists ranging from The Who to Coldplay to Queen. We carefully edited out the worst of the swearing and extreme violence that would land us in trouble

in the wake of the Mirror scandal. We cut the scene which showed three rioters being beaten by our troops behind the wall, not because I disagreed with it but because I felt others might be sickened by it. My commentary was horrendous and during the cut I found it difficult to listen to my voice. I find it traumatic and difficult to relate to unless I'm angry.

Matty was the Producer and Editor and I was the Director. We called ourselves WebLave Productions and I was very proud of my first feature-length film. Matty had also been working solo on a separate project, a comedy filmed in Iraq, which he kept under wraps even from me.

That Saturday we had our own premiere showing in the corporal's bar in front of a drunken audience. I ran mine first on the big screen, expecting lots of praise — but squaddies aren't interested in watching something they had just spent six months doing. So it was just me stood watching on my own. No one else gave a hoot.

"Tunes are good Webby, but the film's fucking wank!" shouted Liam. Next was Matty's turn to show his secret production, which he named Gulf War Syndrome

. It was the funniest film I've ever seen. The lads were in fits of laughter and the music was perfect. I was laughing so much that I forgot about the disappointing reaction to my screening. It was a bit like the popular MTV show Jackass, shot on location in Iraq. At the time there was more concern about that reaching the public that mine.

It wasn't long before I found the original documentary tapes so hard to stomach that I destroyed the three that I had filmed and gave the rest back to the other members of my company. But shortly after the screening there was a spike in interest — I had about 100 orders and could not keep up with the demand. Even the commanding officer and RSM bought two copies each.

Gulf War Syndrome sold out in about an hour.

37. Change Of Pace

By June 2004 I had married the girl I met over leave and we were expecting our first child. I had grown apart from many of my old friends and my priorities had completely changed. Sometimes a fork in the road appears and you've got to go your separate ways.

I felt I needed to get my new family back to Cornwall so I started to think about an Army posting to get more security for my family. I walked into Maj Pearce and Rob Warne's office.

"How soon can you get me a posting out of the regiment Rob?" I asked.

"Tomorrow, is that fast enough?" he replied, "Straight up, Cpl Jones said he doesn't want to go to ATR Winchester in two weeks time. Do you want it?"

I had always wanted that job. As soon as it was confirmed I packed my house and booked my trip out of Germany.

***

The next day the compulsory drug testing team arrived unexpectedly. The blokes were shitting it and with good reason — some of them had been out the previous night, and I knew that there had been a lot of pill taking and cocaine use. I was on that list of people who had to provide a urine sample and my job was to round everyone up and march them to the testing centre. Baxter was also on the list, as were a lot of others I knew would be suspect, which made me think there was a rat in the house.

I was clean but offered Baxter the chance to run or get someone to pee for him. Instead he just got on parade and awaited the call. I felt sorry for him; he was also recently married with a kid on the way and this one stupid mistake was going to cost him and his family dearly. I spoke to Rob Warne about helping him out but he wasn't sympathetic; those two didn't get on after an altercation at a wedding. So it looked like curtains for Baxter.

One week later they printed the names of everyone who had failed the urine test on the notice board for everyone to see. As expected, poor old Bax was up there. His career was over and he would have to find another way to pay the bills.

***

I had packed up my house and was off. The boys had been like brothers to me and it was going to be sad not working with them again. The mortar platoon I had served with since 1998 gave me a send off with a nice Army statue presented by Hoppy and Browny.

As I said my final speech to the young lads who had just joined the platoon, I noticed that many of my old friends had not turned up. Perhaps they were glad I was going. Perhaps I had been a bully and a stickler for duty. Perhaps the time had for me to clear my desk and bugger off.

"Thanks for the statue, this has been my home for a long time and I loved this platoon. Don't let it ever change and keep the spirit alive. Nat, Will, Hoppy, Browny, Pick, Lamby, and Whatty, you keep safe. And may you all lose limbs on your next tours you bunch of Bastards!" I said, to my own amusement.

I walked out the door. That was the last time I ever saw many of them.

38. Learning Curve

I was just about to turn 30 and had a wife and son. My life had changed so dramatically in just four months. Perhaps it was all a bit too much; one minute I'm up to my eyeballs in dead bodies, the next I'm settled down with responsibilities and about to start a high profile job.

Was I ready to do all this? Were all my demons just going to leave me alone? I really didn't know.

ATR Winchester was a shock to the system and I needed to get fit. I would be training 17 to 18 year old Royal Engineers so had to get my shit together. I hadn't lost my temper in a long while and seemed to have calmed down a lot. Maybe I was changing.

The new boss I was working for would not allow me to train recruits until I had completed a course on working with various groups of people in a number of situations. It was called ITCUS but some of my mates had labelled it 'shitcus'. Nevertheless I had to do it to get my own squad and start training.

On the course I met an old Green Jacket mate named Ginge Holden. He was Light Division like me. We were being trained by artillery on infantry skills, which was like the police being trained by special constables on arresting people. It was our field of expertise but we needed the ticks in the book.

On the last two days of the course we had to clean our rifles and hand them in. I had never fired mine and was cleaning away when the Artillery Instructor approached me. He leaned over my shoulder, picked up a piece of my rifle and said that it wasn't clean.

I said "I know — I haven't cleaned it yet."

He made a sarcastic remark about being infantry and not being able to clean the rifle properly. I bit, saying that the weapon was dirty when I got it out.

"Well, I inspected these weapons last time — are you saying I never checked them properly?" he asked angrily.

I wanted to keep quiet… but I let my frustration get the better of me.

"Yes." I said, "You haven't inspected these weapons properly."

"Right, stop whinging and clean your rifle!" he sneered. All week he had assessed us on our tempers to see how we would deal with recruits in tense situations. Now, here was him shouting and swearing at me like I was a piece of shit.

"Now listen pal, you've been banging on about treating recruits with respect, yet you have none of those qualities yourself." I said.

I was calmly given a last warning to clean my weapon and shut up or I would be charged. At this point a Para Sergeant, who was a complete arse licker, piped up. He had been slagging off my regiment already that week. He said:

"Shut the fuck up you hat bastard!"

I slammed my rifle down, shouting obscenities, punched the door open and stormed outside, telling the Para prick to 'fuck off' on my way. The instructor marched on ahead and led me to his room to try and diffuse the situation. I felt bad for losing it and also ashamed — I had a family now and couldn't afford to mess up.

"What was all that about?" asked the instructor.

I burst into tears. I realised for the first time that I had a problem and promised the instructor that I would sort I out.

"Please don't grass me up" I begged.

He said he wouldn't. I had passed the course and finished top of the class. I could have been destined for big things if I could just control my violent temper. It was a big reality check for me as I realised I was no longer in my regiment and no one would cover up for me here. I once nearly beat someone to death in the army and it was all covered up by my fellow soldiers. I had been allowed to get away with it for too long — this had to end now.

Leaving the regiment I grew up in was my biggest challenge. I would have to find a way to negotiate without violence.

In the Light Infantry I was feared but not respected, and that's not a great legacy — in fact I had very few good friends. I was just an angry man with a chip on his shoulder.

39. Fresh Fodder

I passed the course and got back to Winchester where I was given my own section and had to work with an old friend called Pete Judge, who was a platoon sergeant. We went back a long

way being from the same regiment. I went down to the platoon office to meet up with Pete and he introduced me to Ned, a guy from the Royal Tank Regiment.

It was at Winchester that I learned to write reports. I had a teacher help me with my grammar to a standard where I could string a sentence together. Her name was Sonia and I learned so much from this amazing woman who helped many soldiers.

Ned would be showing me the ropes. We got on really well — he had been at Winchester for two years and that experience is invaluable when training civilians to become soldiers. The Platoon Commander was called Mick. He was a warrant officer, not an officer.

We were there to produce soldiers and had put a hard training program together that would prepare them for Iraq or Afghanistan. There were two other corporals who were from the 9th/12th Lancers and the Medical Corps respectively and, in spite of our different backgrounds, we all had to work together to get the job done.

I had the same room that I had when I did my training 10 years previous and it was really strange having my old bed space back. On the day of the recruits' arrival I gave them their beds and had written up some notes for their stay.

I addressed them: "Right lads... I'm Cpl Webster and I'm your dad for the next 12 weeks. If you have joined this for a laugh and think it's going to be easy, then fuck off now.

"I'm a team player and hate ass lickers, bullies, liars, and jack bastards. We work together and we get through it together.

"If you are not interested in killing people then you best leave now because, in truth, we're in the business of fucking folk up with weapons. Any questions? No? Good... Banks, you're my second in command for tonight. Sort your kit out. Tomorrow the fun starts."

***

The training was going well but there were a lot of conflicting training methods. Cpl Stacey and Cpl Caulfield ran their wing very differently and were always trying to outdo the infantry, as we were labeled as thick cannon fodder. Ned was getting out so only came in when he had to, which was rarely. I couldn't blame him; civvy street was his priority. But the other two Corporals were not passing me the necessary information and deliberately getting me in the shit. I had to address it but tact is not my strong point.

It was raining on the rifle range and I was in charge of the lads. I had to organise the range layout for the shoot and distribute ammunition.

"Close in, chimps!" I shouted to the platoon. "Top tip here lads — the weather is shit so get your ammo out of the boxes and, rather than put it in the mud, take your helmets off and keep it in there. Get yourself into some sort of cover and place your rifle magazine in your helmet like

this. Treat it like a new born child as it is your lifeline — the enemy's death will only be achievable with clean ammo" I said whilst demonstrating.

"Stop! Stop!" screamed out Stacey, "Webby what are you doing? You know if the RQMS turns up and sees them putting bullets in their helmets we will get fucked"

"Gents, keep loading up the way I showed you, it keeps the ammo dry and free from the dirt that causes stoppages. Sorry Stacey, can I have a quiet word?" I asked.

I took her to one side and told her that if the RQMS turned up and said something about a technique that could save lives I would take full responsibility for my actions and that it was best to leave me to run the range. I was so wound up with her sticking her nose into my business. I was an experienced infantry soldier and knew my job. Medicine was her area and I would never have interrupted her lessons.

Later, Pete turned up and showed the lads some firing positions that would improve their shooting. These techniques were not in the manual, but we wanted to give our blokes the best chance of survival, so applied what we had learned from experience.

Once again, Stacey had to say her piece. She approached Pete and told him not to fire like that because it wasn't a recognised firing position. A medic telling the infantry how to shoot was madness. I tried to be professional by not showing her up in front of the squad, instead saving my feedback for later.

That afternoon back at the office I thought I would have a word with them. I told Stacey and Caulfield that Pete had served 18 years and seen many conflicts and is one of the best sergeants I knew. I told them that if I tell the lads to load their magazines like I did, and Pete tells them to fire standing a certain way, then they will load and fire like that. I stressed that this was our department, not theirs, and they had no right to interfere.

But Stacey wasn't having it. "What's your problem, Webby?" she snapped. I wasn't about to take a backward step.

"Don't fuck with me Stacey — if you want to act like a bloke I will treat you like a bloke. Don't ever talk down to me in front of my men or I will bite chunks out of your face!"

She started to cry and looked really scared; I hadn't realised how aggressive I was being.

I was ashamed of my behavior to Stacey. I would never have done anything like hit her, but she didn't deserve to be threatened in such a way either. I was the one with an ego and a bad agenda. I needed to sort my life out. An hour later when I calmed down I apologised for my attitude and gave her a hug.

I was right in terms of my teaching methods, though; all of our platoon passed the shoots first time. And that's good.

***

My men were doing great. Smith, Banks, Hughes and Cuthbert had all come so far and bonded really well. On the final exercise I took them out and practised them on rural contact drills at night. They were not supposed to go that far with infantry battle skills but this would give them the edge in Iraq or Afghanistan. I was tough on my Recruit soldiers, but also fair. We did interrogation and escape and evasion. Again, these were not in the crap training package we had to work with, so we added some of our own expertise.

At Christmas 2005 we were at the end of the training. I was really gutted to see them go as they had helped me as much as I had helped them with their careers.

On the last night I was on duty and came into their room with some beers.

"It's not 'Corporal' now — I bloody hate being called that — it's Webby. And you are all soldiers, so here's to all your careers and to keeping safe where ever you serve."

Seeing them pass out the next day was amazing. I was so proud — it was probably one of the best times in my whole career. In my section was the best shot, Sapper Banks, the best recruit, Sapper Smith, and the most improved, Sapper Hughes. All of my boys had done well, and to get the awards proved that I could train recruits and they all knew I had prepared them for anything.

"Good luck boys and thanks for the tankard and vouchers. You all did yourselves proud. Stay low, move fast and trust no one.

"May you live long and have amazing adventures in your Army careers like I did."

Seeing these guys come through and develop really stirred my emotions. I'd had an incredible career as a frontline soldier, but I was a family man now. It was time for me to move on and leave war behind.

It turned out to be the greatest challenge of my life. My real war had only just begun.

40. Breaking News

It was Saturday the 12th of February 2006 and I was at home playing with my child. My wisdom teeth had been removed and I was on a course of very strong painkillers so had been given the week off work.

At about 6pm the phone rang. The caller ID showed it to be a German number.

"Webby, get rid of those DVDs you made — there's been a video clip leaked to the press showing the abuse of Iraqi prisoners. No one really knows what it is but it's going to be on the 10 o'clock news." the caller said anxiously.

"I haven't got any copies left mate." I said calmly. "I sent one to my brother in Italy and one to Stevie Fowell in Weston-super-Mare. Don't worry about it, I cut out all the shit that could get soldiers into trouble."

I was trying to act like I was unfazed but I was actually really worried. That weekend I had lost my good luck rosary beads that my nan gave to me. I had never misplaced them before — they usually went everywhere with me. It wasn't a good sign.

I didn't tell my wife about the phone call because I was worried about how she might react. All night the anxiety built inside me like a volcano. I felt so weak and sick in anticipation of the evening news.

We were sat watching TV when it came on. As usual they announced the main headlines as the theme tune played. Mixed in with the dramatic music I heard my voice commentating on that piece of footage I had shot from the roof. My heart started to pound, beating faster and faster, until I thought it was going to burst out of my chest.

"Oh my god," gasped my wife, "that's your voice!" She started pacing up and down, angry and disappointed and scared all at once. The newsreader announced the top story: British soldiers had been caught on video beating Iraqi civilians.

Although I had not been mentioned by name at this point, the story was on every news channel — CNN, FOX, the internet — everywhere. I, Martin Webster, the simple lad from Falmouth, had just made international headlines.

The phone rang again. This time it was Rob Warne.

"We're in the shit now mate." I said to him in a scared tone. "We need to meet up, we can't speak on this line"

"I know, they're probably watching us right now. Birmingham services, tomorrow, M6, face-to-face... don't get followed" Rob replied.

We both knew we were in trouble, but we needed to get our story together before the police picked us up and tried to turn us against each other. Although I was certain they would never break our bond, I wasn't sure how other members of the battalion would hold out under pressure. Military intelligence would be on us so our circle needed to be tight.

***

That night I had little sleep. I felt guilty that I had let down my new family, my parents and my friends and was concerned with the threat it may pose to them; Muslim extremist groups could have targeted my family for what I'd done.

I wanted to ring Mum and Dad but was too ashamed. All night I was thinking about how I might be publicly torn apart by the media, as had happened when the American abuse photos emerged. It didn't matter that we had been carrying out orders — what mattered was what the public believed. And I no longer had any copies of the whole film to prove our innocence.

As I lay awake looking at my poor wife and child, I started to consider suicide as a way to distance my pathetic existence from them. The few times I did drop off to sleep, I had nightmares where faces of the dead would scare me awake.

I remembered watching the sun rise in Iraq. It felt so positive to be alive. Now any good things we did out there had been destroyed by a 40 second clip.

The clip had shown the public a more accurate picture of the war we were fighting. I was just a silly boy with a video camera who thought it was worth the hype that surrounded it. It wasn't — it was a nightmare that will never leave me.

41. A New Kind Of Battle

As I watched the curtains in my army quarter grow lighter with day break, I realised I was more scared of the media and general public than I had been of any enemy in Iraq. I got up and went downstairs. On the doormat was the News of the World

. There was a still from my video on the front page showing one of my best mates holding a stick in his hand punishing an Iraqi. As I picked it up to read, my wife appeared at the top of the stairs.

"So it wasn't a dream!" she said with her head in her hands.

"Sorry, I've got to go… if the cops come for me, say I'm visiting a relative" I said. In a way I wasn't sure that I would be coming back.

"Don't you leave me on my own with this" she said. She knew deep down that I was contemplating suicide to protect them from the media storm.

That was hard to hear, knowing my wife wanted me there… It would have been easier if she wanted me gone.

***

As I hit the motorway I felt so worthless that I wished for a lorry to crash into my car and crush me to death. I reached my destination I pulled into the car park and saw Rob, a beast of a man leaning against his car with a huge handlebar moustache and mass of curly hair. It was such a morale boost to have him there to talk to.

"Hello, retard boy!" Rob greeted me. I raised a smile but was too withdrawn to laugh.

We got in his car and I sparked up a fag and took a huge drag. "Listen mate we are in the shit big time. How many years do you think we'll get?"

"About five years in Belmarsh Prison I reckon. You'll be Abu Hamza's rent boy and he's going to stick his hook right up your arse!" Rob scoffed. This time I did laugh.

"This is crazy — you look like you're on the run" I commented in reference to his appearance.

"I feel like it. I'm supposed to get my pension in a week's time and I've started my civilian life after 24 years' service. I'm well in the poop"

I told Rob how sorry I was for filming the incident.

"Listen mate — I bought a copy of that film and so did most of the battalion so we're all to blame. I'm just going to tell the press about the shit we were catching. What we did was nothing compared to what we faced."

We didn't talk for long but it was good to know we were in it together.

***

I drove through the afternoon into the evening and as the rain became heavier I started thinking those horrible thoughts again. I saw a bridge in the distance that seemed to invite me towards it. I started to speed up and wanted badly to smash right into the brickwork and end it all there. But then thoughts of my innocent family at my grave started to filter into my head.

Bump-bump-bump-bump!

I snapped out of my trance to find my car gliding over the hard shoulder alarm bumps, meters from death. I swerved back onto the road.

My phone went. It was my friend Tristan McGee.

"Are you okay mate?" he asked.

"No mate, I'm not. I fucked up everything for my family and friends and the Army" I said.

"Listen pal — just think of your family and pull yourself together. People who don't know you will not understand the situation"

I thanked him for the chat and got home as fast as I could. It may have been the phone call that saved my life.

***

I was changing my child's nappy at about 10 o'clock that Sunday evening when the doorbell rang. I knew who it would be. I gave my child to my wife, took a deep breath and opened the door. There were four of them dressed in sharp black suits. The dark-haired copper standing directly in front of me piped up.

"I'm Staff Sgt Hayes, SIB, and we have a search warrant for this property" In they walked. I sat on the couch and Hayes read me my rights.

I was being arrested on suspicion of causing affray during Operation Telic 3 in March 2004. There was little I could say or do. I became withdrawn but wasn't as scared as I thought I would be — I was almost relieved that I had been caught. I knew they had a job to do, just like I was doing mine when following orders without question.

"Can you search my child's room first? We need to let him sleep" I pleaded. But Sgt Hayes seemed unconcerned with my request.

More Feds started to move in and set up an ICP while one woman logged and reported areas to search. This time it wasn't just the Royal Military Police doing some half-assed search for a broken CD used as a weapon. The SIB would leave no stone unturned. They told me the search could take hours and that I would be taken to Aldershot to be interviewed for up to two days.

My wife was going mental, calling them bastards for not allowing our child to go to bed. They trashed the house in pursuit of DVDs and video tapes. They took our computer and cameras and any recording equipment. Even our wedding photos were confiscated.

At the end of the search I said sorry and goodbye to my wife. I had tried to remain calm and started to think of what, if anything, I would say when interviewed. I sat in the back of their car as they tried to negotiate the route out of Worthy Down and back to Aldershot but they got lost and I had to give them directions to the M4. Apparently the thick twats had never heard of a road map. I would hate to have been sent on operations with these guys.

42. From Soldier To Prisoner

It was about 3 o'clock in the morning. I was shattered and running on pure adrenaline, petrified about how my wife might be feeling. Yet as much guilt as I felt I was sort of switching off to what was going on around me.

"Stand on the yellow line and strip your clothes off" said the duty copper.

I had been sent to a Royal Logistical Core camp jail to be locked up for the night before the interview with the Special Investigation Branch the following day. The duty Provo Corporal was treating me as if I was a terrorist, even though he was the same rank as me — some fuckwit who got his stripes through walking dogs. Two SIB cops were overlooking the personal search.

"What are these tablets for?" the corporal asked.

"Pain killers — I've just had my wisdom teeth out"

"You're under our detention tonight and you play by my rules — understand?" he barked.

"Yes" I said quietly.

"Yes staff!" he shouted. The jumped-up little prick was insisting I respect him. I stared him in the eyes with my hands behind my back and could feel my blood boil.

"Right, follow me" said the REMF as the SIB walked off. It was as if they had told him to fuck me around.

"There's your bedding. Make your bed. There's the buzzer if you need a piss. When you lie on the bed do not lie on your side — you are to have your head in the upright position at all times. I will check on you every hour through this hatch. Do you understand?" the Corporal yelled.

"Yes" I again said quietly.

"Yes staff!" he said abruptly. I turned my back on him and started to make my bed.

"Oi! I'm talking to you dickhead!" he roared.

I turned around and replied "What?" in a teasy manner.

"Don't push your luck with me son" he said, then turned and walked out in a huff.

I wasn't playing the game anymore. I was no longer a member of the British Army. They were turning on each other and I had been captured by the enemy.

At 4 o'clock a bang woke me up. It was my old buddy the corporal again making sure I hadn't dozed off.

"Oi, fuckwit, get your head up!" he shouted angrily. I was now really starting to get pissed off with this… but I had to stay focused. I had big decisions to make. What do I do? Do I admit it and finger my mates who were involved in the beating? Do I say 'no comment' and wait until the trial? Or do I give these cocks some false leads to send them on a wild goose chase and buy us all some time?

5 o'clock and another bang on the cell door; "I won't tell you again — get your head up or I will take your bedding." This

time I got out of bed and started to pace up and down the cell, starting to put a story together in my head.

6 o'clock came and I had made the bed up with pillows as though I was sleeping on my side. Bang went the shutter as it fell down.

"Oi! wake up!" the cock shouted while I hid behind the door. When he opened the door to look inside I flew towards the bed and shouted "Boo!"

He wasn't impressed to say the least, telling me to get out and have a shave.

43. Scapegoat

As I washed I could hear the news on in the guard room. There was a new provo sergeant taking over from the prick corporal. I was called out and made to stand on the yellow line while we went through the prisoner hand over routine.

The new sergeant said, "At ease — let's get some scoff"

I followed him to the cook house. The radio was on and the soldiers in there eating their breakfast were all staring at me. The news came on and I understood why.

"News report; After the News of the World Iraqi abuse video footage, Army Intelligence have arrested a 29-year-old male who is being detained in police custody in Aldershot. Details are scarce."

It was so weird. I grabbed as much breakfast as I could. I needed to fuel up and get my act together.

"Did you do it?" asked the sergeant.

"Yes," I admitted "but no one knows how much shit we had taken before that clip."

As we walked back to the jailhouse he said "A little advice… tell them pigs nothing. They're going to hang someone for this mate."

He was sound as fuck, this guy. He told me there were a paper and some fags in the room and I wasn't going back to the cell until the police got there. I had an opportunity to use the phone now and ring my wife. To show my appreciation I offered my hand and said "Thank you so much, I'll never forget this."

He simply said "British soldiers should stick together pal, no problems." It was a pity some of my mates didn't think like that.

I went to use the phone and caught a glimpse of GMTV. They were setting up a phone-in (civvies will make a buck out of any situation). I started to read the texts and emails received by the TV station as they were shown across the bottom of the screen.

'These soldiers are a disgrace to the nation and should go to prison for 10 years and have their pensions withdrawn'

read one. At first I thought it must have been one of my mates who had written that for a laugh. I was genuinely gutted at what I was reading and how the media was sensationalising the issue.

I called my wife.

"Rob's been on the phone all night making sure I'm okay. Don't tell those bastards anything. No one's on our side now. Do what you have to do" she said.

Throughout the call I kept touching my wedding ring. It was at this point I realised how much I cared for my family and it gave me purpose to go on living. They were all that mattered.

That was the green light for me; As soon as the call ended I started to write my story down on paper. Then I went outside for a fag in the courtyard and went over it again and again. Every hour I had before the interview was vital to beating my new enemy, the SIB.

***

It was time to go and I was ready for these bastards now. I met with my solicitor from Foster and Wells. She was young but seemed quite clever and I had time to gather my plea for the recorded interview that afternoon.

"Did you film it?" she said.

"No I couldn't have, I was on the ground level at all times. I know of other guys filming and I can give their names" I replied. I knew filming wasn't illegal so I could give names of other guys who were filming knowing that none of them were responsible for the scandalous footage. I thought this might give the soldiers who gave the kicking time to sort their shit out as it would only be a matter of time before they were tracked down. No one was on our side, so I had to do what I could by fair means or foul.

Staff Sergeant Hayes, The man who had arrested me, was the interviewing officer and had a right smug look about him. The interview started and I managed to go along with it without mentioning Rob Warne or Maj Pearce.

"Martin, we're coming to the end of the tape so will have to take a break" said Hayes. "We have already interviewed Cpl Williams and Sgt Major Head from Milan platoon. We know you're covering for Rob Warne and Maj Pearce, so during the break I suggest you rethink your statement"

Over a fag I had a chat with my solicitor. I knew they had me about Rob Warne. I was thinking to myself, 'why has Head given us up? They've fucked up everything now, what happened to sticking together?'

We sat down for the second half of the interview.

"You do realise you could get into heaps of trouble if you're hiding something Martin? You said to Cpl Williams of Milan platoon in the cook house that you filmed the beating that took place in the palace" he said.

"No, what I said to Cpl Williams is that I saw a scuffle from the front entrance of the palace with Rob and Womble by the main gate and it looked like they were kicking something. I could not see what they were kicking as my line of sight from that level was obscured by a podium... they could have been kicking each other or a curb" I said calmly.

Hayes responded quickly to my answer by asking the time and date of when I saw this.

"It was two years ago. In case you didn't realise, there was a war going on" I said sarcastically.

"So you saw Rob and Womble kicking an Iraqi on the ground?" Hayes said, starting to get agitated.

"Is that what I just said? No, listen; I don't know what they were kicking. There was a lot going on and I would rather not go over it again and again"

"Why Martin — are you covering for someone? Has Rob Warne threatened you? We have evidence that he has tried to get hold of you and we believe you are covering for him and Maj Pearce."

I said nothing. I had lost all respect for the Army, the UK and the war. I was no longer on the same side as Hayes.

"Right Martin we are going to show you a series of clips so that you can tell us which ones you filmed" Hayes said. He was watching my body language and trying to work me out. He knew I was lying but if the politicians who run our country could get away with it, then so could I.

He showed me a series of clips. Some I had filmed but a lot were unfamiliar.

"I recognise some of the areas like the Pink Palace, but I don't recognise the blokes in any of the clips. Sorry I can't help you on this occasion"

"That's your voice though?" he said.

"What voice?" I asked innocently.

"The voice on the camera! Cpl Webster you could get sent down for a long time if you keep protecting your superiors" I had clearly riled him. But I wasn't budging.

"I'm telling you — it was a long time ago when I made that DVD, but none of that shit was on my tapes."

To my relief the interview ended. As I waited in the corridor I overheard Hayes and his goons talking about my house search.

"Boss, we found nothing on the video tape, the DVDs were blank and the hard drive was clean" said one. Hayes then called me back to the interview room — he had good and bad news.

"You're being released without charge, but the MOD press office are hassling us for details to release your name to the media. It's getting released tonight at 7 o'clock"

"What? But you haven't charged me with anything and you're letting me go!"

"It's 6 o'clock now, if I was you I'd get your family out of Winchester and go into hiding as the media are going to hunt you down" Hayes said.

"Are the Army press at least going to say I have been released without charge?" I asked.

Hayes said he didn't know before turning his back on me.

44. Trial By Media

I was so drained by now but I had only half an hour before they released my details to the world. They had arranged military transport for me and the driver kindly let me use his phone so I could ring my wife.

"We have to leave for Cornwall tonight. In fact we have one hour before the media are going to be looking for us" I said.

"Why aren't the Army protecting us?"

"Because they don't give a toss. We're on our own now, we need to go home and hide for about ten days until the media storm blows over" I said.

She was very upset and justifiably so. This was her worst nightmare and it was all my fault. But I had to stay focused; I was about to become infamous and had no media training to help me weather the storm.

I rang my father at 7.30pm.

"Dad it's Martin — do you know what's happened?" I asked him.

"Do I know what's happened? The whole bloody world knows what's happened," he said, "You don't do things small boy, do you?"

I apologised to him and mum and asked them not to speak to the media, or if they had no alternative to just say 'no comment.' I told dad I was on my way to Cornwall and would come and visit when it had blown over.

***

I got home to find my wife had packed the cars and was waiting with our child ready to leave. That night we drove in separate cars, stopping only twice to feed our baby. I chain smoked and listened to reports on the radio about my video footage. As we sped through Taunton we both got flashed by speed cameras. I wondered if anything else could go wrong.

We arrived at my wife's sister's house at 4 o'clock in the morning. Our plan was to stay there for a few days with her and her husband so that no one would find us. I went to a pay phone to make a call to my old army friend from the Northern Ireland days, Steve Fowell. It was late but I knew he could help me.

"Steve, I'm in the shit big time. You need to contact the News of the World and show them the DVD I sent you, show them what really happened. I will ring again in couple of days" I said hurriedly.

That was all I had to do; he was a true friend and had the know-how to be my 'Spin Doctor.'

The papers were well and truly after my scalp and I couldn't bring myself to read any more headlines. At this point I was also taking anti-depressants that I had managed to get hold of.

45. Facing The Firing Squad

The next day I saw that the local news had shown my mum and dads' home on the TV, giving enough details for any terrorist cell to use. The

Falmouth Packet,

the local paper that I had loved since I was a kid and had been sent out to me on many operational tours, had completely torn me to bits. It seemed everyone was searching for dirt on me. I was devastated when I saw my parents' address printed on the front page.

The phone rang and it was the Adjutant.

"Where are you staying Cpl Webster?" he asked.

"I'm not going to disclose that information, sir." I said in a distressed voice.

"You need to come back immediately"

"I can't, I need to protect my family"

"Listen Cpl Webster, you are a British soldier and you must return for work tomorrow morning so come and see me. If you do not turn up we will post you as AWOL." he ordered. I had the same questions on a loop in my head; 'Why aren't they protecting us? Why are they treating me like this?'

My wife was really angry at me and I broke down in tears. I couldn't handle it anymore. She walked away and her brother-in-law was really kind and told me to be strong and go back to sort this mess out.

I sat up and prepared my car for the journey while my sister-in-law made me tea. I said goodbye to them all. At least I knew that they were safe at that house and no one could hurt them. I was very grateful to my sister-in-law and her husband. They will never know how much it helped.

***

I drove through the night and arrived at Winchester at about 4am. The house was full of our possessions, including an empty cot where my baby usually slept. I broke down again. It was as if karma was saying 'what goes around comes around'.

That morning I went to meet my OC Maj Edmonds and Capt Armstrong. They were so good to me and offered their full support for me to stay at ATR Winchester training recruits. We walked to the CO's office but he was away so Maj Ramsey from the RGBW was running the camp.

"March in and salute him" Capt Armstrong said in an encouraging tone. I was sleep-deprived, weak and altogether had had enough of Army bullshit and wasn't in the mood for people treating me like something they'd trodden in.

I walked in and took one look at the red-faced fossil staring back at me and could tell that things weren't going to go well.

"Are you Cpl Webster?" he sneered.

"Yes Sir" I stood vacantly gazing at the paperwork he had on the table.

"So you are the man who has brought shame on his camp and dishonoured this regiment. What were you thinking of when selling that to the News of the World?"

"I didn't sell it sir, I haven't been charged yet" My legs were shaking. I barely had the energy to stand.

"Why can't you stand up straight, boy? What's wrong with you!" he bellowed. I didn't answer. There was no point.

"I don't want you here," he said, "you will be cross posted to the Royal Green Jackets from today"

"But sir, 1RGJ are in Blackpool and my wife is in Cornwall and very ill at the moment. Both regiments are deploying to Iraq, I love it here and I'm going to be a recruiting sergeant in 6 months at Taunton"

"Well you should have thought of that before you made the video — now get out!"

As I walked out I could feel my career being taken from me. I loved my job training recruits — it was the best one I'd ever had. I burst into tears again and bowed my head in shame. Two weeks earlier, I had seen 'Sgt Webster' penciled in for Taunton recruiting centre. I had my young family, we were just about to buy a house — everything seemed to be going so perfect up until the phone call I received telling me that my video was going to be on the news. I had it all and lost it all in a moment.

Captain Armstrong put his arm around my shoulder and said "Come on son, cheer up... don't let him get you down. Me and Maj Edmonds are going to get you that posting to 2RGJ down at Bulford so that you're closer to your wife and child. You're one of our best NCOs and we're gutted to lose you but you will pull through."

Gratefully, I said "Thanks Sir, that means a lot and I won't forget what you and Maj Edmonds have done for me."

Maj Ramsey had given me a week to pack my house and get my stuff out of there. I had to drive to Bulford and meet my new OC down at the Royal Green Jackets the next day.

46. The Royal Green Jackets

As soon as I entered the battalion cook house on my first day at 2RGJ I could see that the regiment had some problems. All the black lads from Jamaica, St Lucia, and Sierra Leone were seated on one side of the room, all the white lads from London, Birmingham, Manchester and Liverpool were sitting on the other and in the middle was a huge tribe of Fijians, with their chief at the end of the table. And then there was me, an outcast from all three groups. As I walked past the huge divisions towards the main queue many people were staring at me as they knew I was the guy that filmed the beating. On top of that, my cap badge was a Light Infantry bugle with red backing — and the 'chosen men' hate red back bastards. I was shitting myself.

"Webster! You mad wanker" boomed a voice from behind me. I turned around to see it was Wig, my good friend from the Light Infantry. He had been kicked out like me — it seemed they sent all rogues and reprobates to the Jackets.

"Mate, am I glad to see you!" I said with great relief. I knew Wig was a right hard bastard and good in a tight spot if I was going to get trouble.

"Come sit with me. I heard you were coming and I've sorted out your room" he said.

I followed him over to the Fijians' table where about four big guys stood up to shake my hand. I responded promptly.

"These boys have taken me under their wing, no one fucks with me. I do my own shit here" said Wig.

Wig got kicked out of 1LI for one too many fights. The last straw was one night in the Corporal's mess where he punched five or six different corporals in the face for no other reason than he had lost the plot. It took for Jay Davies to wrap a wooden deck chair around his head to stop him. But he was a fantastic ally who could possibly stop me getting ass-fucked in the shower.

***

On my way to my room I bumped into another mate from the Green Jackets, Colin Cope.

"You're coming out with me tonight Webster, you legend. Great film!" he said. I was feeling much better — I had two friends here now as opposed to the zero I had when I arrived. As I was putting my kit in my room I recognised a familiar face in the room next door — it was Trapper, our sniper from Iraq.

"I got interviewed three times about you and that video" he said.

"Bloody police will be coming back to me soon, too. I've seen Rob Warne and we are sticking to the same story. The police weren't out there in Iraq when we were getting hammered by rioters, rifles and grenades, so fuck them. How have you coped since coming back to your regiment?"

"Not well mate — I tried to strangle the Sergeant Major when I got no leave after coming back from war. They think I've lost it and give me a wide berth now"

"Do the people here know that you've killed more people than cancer?" I said laughing.

"I don't give two shits what they think they know" Trapper replied bluntly.

47. Flashback

That night Colin, my Green Jacket friend, knocked on my door and we went out for drinks. We talked about civvy street and told old stories of 1LI and how the Army had changed for the worse.

When we got into a taxi to come back, the song playing on the radio made me feel strange. I had heard it loads of times but the road we were on travelling back from Salisbury seemed to remind me of Iraq.

The song was Elton John and that crap boy band Blue, and it was triggering a strange flash back. Until this point in my life I had never experienced anything like it. It was to be the first of many.

In my head I was back in Iraq on the notorious Route 6 between Basra and Amarah...

"Right Webby"

Jono was saying, "you push your road cut-off team about 300 meters south but stay in radio range. I will wait up here with the decoy and set up a vehicle check point with the Iraqi police. As soon as you see an approaching vehicle turn away suspiciously, do what you got to do to stop them"

Me and Jono had devised this cunning plan to stop dodgy vehicles and bandits turning around at the VCPs to avoid detection. This time we would have some silent assassins waiting for them.

"Okay Jono, I will only need Browny"

I said excitedly. I loved working with small numbers and Browny was a superb soldier. Not the fittest but experienced, powerful and intelligent which in the infantry can be rare. He also had a wicked sense of humour.

As we were setting up, the first vehicle approached our location and began to slow down. The VCP was waving a red light in a circular motion to get the car to stop. Jono was sending us sit reps. Browny was on the other side of the road and we were talking to each other in a jovial manner as Qalat Salih's street lamps twinkled in the night sky.

"We got another customer"

said Browny in a stupid American accent.

This time the car was approaching fast and didn't seem to slow. All of a sudden it slowed down to about 20 mph as it had obviously clocked the road block ahead waving the red torch. We waited until the vehicle had passed us, lying in the ditches like wolves stalking their pray.

"Get ready, Browny"

I whispered.

We had earlier planned how we were going to stop the vehicles, and it was going to be very different to Northern Ireland where we used road spikes and quoted the 'N.I. Emergency Provisions Act' while some Paddy told us to fuck off. Hard, fast and aggressive was how we would achieve our aim.

The vehicle ground to a halt and turned off its lights. It span around with great haste, wheels spinning and spraying dust and small stones everywhere. It was now 15 to 20 metres away and gathering speed.

"Go, go, go!"

We moved swiftly into the centre of the road and cocked our weapons, both concentrating our sights firmly on the driver's head. If need be, a cluster of lead would disengage his thoughts from his foot on the accelerator pedal and bring the vehicle to a halt.

The vehicle stopped dead and the silence was broken by us screaming;

"Get the fuck out of the vehicle now! Get out!"

The hands of the two in the front seat went up immediately. The person in the back had his hands under his ass and looked shit-scared.

"Browny you do the man in the back, I will take these two out"

I shouted.

The two blokes in the front were under my guidance and I was using the end of my gun as a pointer with my eye an inch away from the sight, ready to take that shot at any second.

"Over there, over there!"

I pointed to the side of the road. They followed my instructions so I was able to check out Browny's situation

"I think this guy is a suicide bomber — he won't get out the car

!" shouted Browny, agitated. But I knew he could handle it.

"Down, face out!"

I yelled, putting the men's hands behind their heads and sitting them apart from each other facing opposite directions.

"Get out of the fucking car or I'm going to kill you!"

screamed Browny at the top of his lungs. He was getting really mad but the guy still wouldn't cooperate.

'What is it he sat on

,' I thought, 'are they going to blow us all up?'

Then Browny shouted, "Cover me!"

and slung his rifle over his back. He climbed into the car and grabbed the Iraqi around the neck, dragging him out.

"Fucking hell,"

Browny said, "it's a suicide vest!" I reacted quickly, grabbing the bloke and pulling him violently towards the other Iraqis so that I had control of all three.

By this point Jono had turned up and we had more men on the ground. Browny leant into the car and carefully popped open a pocket on the ammo belt. Bandits would often stuff the cotton ammo pouches with semtex plastic explosives, nuts, bolts and nails to create makeshift suicide vests. Luckily that was not the case on this occasion.

"It's okay... it's just AK47 magazines and bullets"

he said, then reached under the seats and pulled out two AK47 assault rifles. This would later validate our stop and search as carrying guns in motor cars is not allowed in Iraq. Jono also found a 9mm pistol in the glove compartment. These guys were either bandits or planning to kill someone that night.

We wrapped up the search and drove the car back to the cop shop in Qalat Salih. As we got in the car Asad, our interpreter, dished out the fags. I was in the passenger seat and Curly was driving. Browny was in the back spraying air freshener at Asad's Face.

This was probably one of the most surreal moments of my time in Iraq. I started to tune the radio in and I got BFBS. And that shit song by Blue and Elton John started playing.

"What I got to do to make you love me! What I got to do to make you care!"

we all sang together. Even Asad tried to join in but with his wailing Iraqi voice he couldn't hit the high notes like us Brits... Back in reality our taxi had arrived back at Bulford Camp. Everyone ran over to the kebab van. I just stayed quiet. This experience of flashbacks was to have a profound effect on my life and how I changed.

I couldn't sleep all night. I was suffering from Post-Traumatic Stress Disorder and the battle had only just begun.

48. Muslims Are Not Your Enemy

The next morning I met my new boss Capt Rob Cutler. He was what we call in the trade 'a ranker' having worked his way up from Rifleman to Captain. They are given the highest respect. He seemed really relaxed and told me he had passed out with Rob Warne and to pass on his regards. This was another good start and I promised Cutler I would work very hard for him. I had to convert the whole Battalion to FV432 armoured vehicle in six months and I was the only man on camp that could instruct on the tanks.

So I was my own boss and soon had my own classroom and free reign to set up the training programme. It wasn't long before the work became too much and I needed a right hand man. So Cutler found me one.

"This is Rfn Missisoee and he will be working for you" said Cutler. I looked the guy up and down and shook his hand.

"Alright mate, I'm Webby. Let's go down to my garage and set up the 432s for teaching next week" I said. He looked quite young and reminded me of Muhammad Ali in his youth.

"Call me Z. I heard you got kicked out your old regiment. What was wrong with the Light Infantry?" he enquired.

"Fuck all, they just don't want me back and I want out" I said. Z looked surprised at my attitude. He was obviously holding back and not really relaxed around me.

The next day Z and one of his mates came down to the garage to help clean and prepare the tank for next week's lessons.

"So what's Iraq like Webby?" asked Z.

"It's full of Muslims and they are the most ungrateful bastards I have ever met. In fact I hate them and will never serve for this country ever again"

"Did you film that beating of those kids?"

"Yes I did, but if you were out there getting days and days of grenades, bullets and RPGs fired at you morning, noon and night, you'd soon see if you would put up with that shit. We are supposed to be helping them become democratic"

Z started to laugh loudly and so did Perezza, his mate.

"What's so funny?" I asked nervously.

"Z's a Muslim!" said Perezza.

I had put my foot in it.

"Sorry mate but that's the way I feel. When you boys go over there you will see what a bunch of twats they all are." I was trying to backtrack a bit but still wanted to get my opinion across. Z stayed quiet, which only made it worse because I kept talking. The more shite I spoke the more Z just stared; not angry, just a look that said he was totally in control and I wasn't. In short, I ended up looking a bit of a dick.

"Listen bro, how long have you been in the army?" he finally asked.

"About 11 years"

"And do you love the Army?"

"I used to. I really did." I said with a touch of remorse.

"Why don't you love the Army now and why do you want to leave?"

"Because the Army wasn't there when I needed it. They sent me to war then charged me for how I behaved in conflict" I said.

"So why is that the fault of the Muslims?"

It was a good question.

"Because those pricks were chucking grenades at us" I said indignantly. Z stayed composed and cool.

"And what would you do if Muslims invaded Cornwall, took over your town, took your infrastructure away and told you how to live?"

"I would fight back with all my might…"

I shut up for a moment to think. Z had a good argument — I admit that. He really did. But the bottom line was that he had not been there yet and hadn't had grenades and such chucked at him by fanatics who he was supposedly trying to help. "You wait, son. When you Jackets get out there, see if you

want to hug the little shits" I said. "I'm not saying they're not little shits for one minute; I'm sure they are, it's just that it's not the Muslims taking you to court — it's this glorious nation you protect and serve" argued Z. I apologised to Z if I had offended him and we shook hands.

"Bro," he said, "you could never offend me!"

The next day, instead of working, me and Z talked more about things. I was slowly growing to really like this lad and realise he was an inspiration to be with. I was still cautious and a little in fear of him due to his faith, but this was a common side effect of going to war in Iraq and the whole media spin.

Z worked hard with me and there was no stopping us. We would finish early on Fridays and bunk off the fitness program to go home early. We had it sorted and were hanging out together everywhere.

One day in the cook house one of the lance corporals came up to me with some advice.

"You see that black prick you're hanging around with?" he said. I looked up. "That gobby Muslim bastard beat up two corporals in a room one night —

one came away with a punctured spleen and the other had a lung damaged. They both went to jail because Z said it was a racially motivated attack" said the squaddie.

"What, Z just went up to them and did that unprovoked?" I asked, surprised.

"No — they went into his room to sort him out, and he got away with it as it was self defence" he said angrily.

"So they deserved it then" I said with a sick grin.

"No, that nigger played the race card like they all do and he got away with mashing up two good lads" he said, clearly frustrated that I wasn't taking his side.

I didn't take the bait. "Well, if two pricks came into my room to fuck me up, I would kill them."

"I'm just warning you, mate — stay away from Z as he's trouble. If you hang around with him, the whites won't like it."

I was beginning to get angry and have thoughts of ripping this guy's windpipe out so turned to leave. The more people told me I couldn't hang around with him the more I saw him as an ally. We were both outcasts and had to stick together.

"I will hang around with anyone I please — understand?" I said. I wanted to make it absolutely clear that no one would tell me what to do.

Already Z was going up in my estimation; I could identify with any man who used violence to protect himself.

49. The New Enemy

On the morning of April 3 2006 I had an interview with Maj McEvoy, another ranker and RGJ legend, about leaving the Army. He was impressed with my record and not judging me solely by my fuck-up in Iraq.

"So," he said, "tell me your reasons for getting out, Cpl Webster"

"Well sir, where do I start? I have lost my promotion and the posting to Taunton I wanted so that I could be closer to my wife. I have the media pursuing me like a dog and the MOD has told the press more than they've told me. And I no longer fully believe in the war and refuse to go out there again as I'm still paying for the last mess. Besides, you're all deploying next February and I want out before then. I will continue to fulfil my duties to the best of my ability and work my ass off until I leave, you have my word"

Maj McEvoy asked what I would do for employment upon leaving the forces and I said I would be getting into the swimming pool business with my father.

"Well in my opinion it's a great loss. I guarantee once this court martial is over you would do really well with the Green Jackets" he said.

"Sir, exactly why am I being tried like a war criminal?"

"I personally don't agree with the way this has been handled and have spoken in great length to Maj Pearce who speaks very highly of you. I can't see what they will achieve with an expensive court martial" he said sternly.

As I walked out of the company offices, I saw my name on the notice board for a course on the new 432 modifications. I was fine with this, as it would keep me busy and make the last year go quickly so that I could put the court martial to one side.

***

I was travelling home to Falmouth for my brother's wedding when Chris Hill, my solicitor, rang to tell me the police wanted to re-interview me that Saturday.

"Not a chance," I told him, "I have a wedding to attend and I'm not under arrest or being charged so I'm definitely going. Fuck Staff Hayes and his shit investigation."

Chris Hill was a top solicitor and knew his law. He said he would see what he could do. He was a very polite and courteous man who knew how to get results and I felt very lucky to have him on my side.

Later I got a call back from Chris.

"Martin, look; they're not happy with your wedding plans but are willing to compromise for Sunday afternoon at 1300 hours" he told me.

Fucking wankers. That meant no drinking at the wedding, plus it would spoil the occasion for me because I'd have it hanging over my head. I'd probably be in a foul mood afterwards and want to kick off. Not the best frame of mind to be in when interviewed by the police.

***

As I drove through the night toward my home in Cornwall, I experienced another flashback, drifting back to Amarah where we had just got back from protecting the palace and were packing our kit to leave Abu Naji.

Jono came into our tent and called us all together.

"You're not going to like this but SIB want to interview Webby, Browny, Benny, Lamby, Pick and Caz for killing that Iraqi from the palace roof on the first night"

he said, shaking his head with disbelief.

We could not believe what we were hearing; we were in a country on the brink of civil war and the police wanted to play good cop bad cop with us.

Benny asked when.

"Now! So get your stories together and remember the yellow card"

Jono said.

"But we're in Iraq, not Northern bloody Ireland!"

Lamby said sarcastically.

"Just play the game lads, these pricks want scalps for the high body count down town"

I said.

The interview room was set up in the Christian chapel. We were taken in two at a time but then separated. Interviewer

Staff Jackmond said he would be asking a lot of in-depth questions on various incidents from that night.

As I took Jackmond through the night's escapades, he listened in disbelief to what we had achieved despite poor ammo scales and lack of military intelligence during the mission. I had to explain the roof top situation in detail to him and he wrote down the notes on his report sheets. This guy had just flown in and had not experienced any of the intense combat. He was struggling to comprehend what we'd been through.

"You say you were on the roof and were having a cigarette with Andy Buller and Jono when you saw, coming up the street from about 150 to 200 meters away, three militia with weapons?" said the SIB man.

"Yes that's right"

I responded.

"How did you know they were militia?"

"Because they all had weapons. It was about 3 o'clock in the morning and no one was around. We had also been under fire all night, so there was probably a good chance they weren't on their way to turn themselves in or join our team"

"You said to me that you moved into a position on the wall and had time to take well aimed shots… you waited for him to bring his weapon to bear?"

he said. I corrected him straight away.

"No, I said I moved into a position that provided me with the best cover from the enemy so that I would not be silhouetted on the top of the palace roof"

I could see that he was trying to manipulate my words to get a conviction. Unlike civilian law, the military police are allowed to use unrecorded interviews as evidence, which meant that my innocence may have relied on his hand-written notes.

"Yes, and it was at that point that you fired nine or ten rounds at his main torso

and he dropped straight away. Is that right Cpl Webster?"

he probed.

"No. I noticed he had brought his weapon to bear in our general direction and was about to commit an offence that was likely to endanger myself or the lives of my fellow soldiers, and at this point I made the decision to use my rifle to eliminate the threat. I fired more rounds at the target's torso and head area but stopped once I perceived the threat to be no more"

I said, quoting the Northern Ireland yellow card.

"Did you not issue a challenge?"

he said very quickly.

"I had no time to issue anything or lives would have been lost on our side. Besides, the rule of a challenge before you fire your rifle in Northern Ireland is to shout 'Army, stop or I will fire', which would be totally useless because he probably didn't speak English."

It was frustrating that he was using this against me, as we had no rules of engagement for Iraq.

"Was his rifle definitely pointed at you and your section?"

"Yes"

"And you only fired aimed shots?"

"Yes!"

I hoped he would take the hint and empathise with me.

"Don't you think that 10 rounds is a little excessive?"

"No, because he was still alive when we brought him back to camp to be searched. If we had 7.62mm, instead of a poxy 5.56mm that do not kill, then we would have probably only needed to fire five to six well aimed shots"

I said.

"Well we're not here to discuss ammo calibre, we are here to investigate the high numbers of so-called militia you shot several nights ago."

The SIB officer was not impressed with my attitude and was getting nowhere.

After six hours of being interviewed I was free to go. As I walked out I met with Jono and we went for a brew and couldn't believe that the interview had even taken place...

I awoke from my dream-like state very angry. The Iraq tour was really starting to play on my mind and I was finding it very difficult to put it behind me. It was making me bitter about my situation. I needed to calm down as it was affecting me and, more importantly, my family. But I was heading home to Cornwall, the one place where I felt safe.

The Military Police had really got to me. I wanted to trust them but their whole ethos was to finger somebody and send them down to earn promotion — a bonus culture based on stabbing soldiers in the back. Not the same code of ethics as a normal soldier.

50. No Comment

After a great family wedding I drove back that Sunday absolutely raging with anger. I remember punching my steering wheel as hard as I could for the duration of the journey, imagining it was Hayes' face. By the time I arrived at Bulford, my knuckles were bleeding, the steering wheel was buckled and I had lost my voice from screaming profanities. I took three antidepressants — partly to get off my trolley so I would be of no use to them, but also to help relax me as my anger was becoming uncontrollable.

Chris Hill was there to meet me and was in good spirits. He cheered me up with some of the other cases in the past he had dealt with and tried to reassure me.

"Good weekend, Martin?" Sgt Hayes said. "I hear you have signed off. That's sad. Sorry to hear about your posting" He must have been being polite in front of my solicitor as it was a completely different demeanour to the one he'd had last time I saw him. I didn't bother responding.

I spoke very little and had a dictaphone secretly placed in my jacket so that I could later refer to anything I said. Chris and I had a brief chat in a separate room from the interrogators to discuss tactics.

"I'm going to say 'no comment' all the way Chris. I've nothing to lose now and don't give a shit who's grassed on me or what they're going to do. I'm going to prepare myself for a stretch in prison. My career's over, my name's shit worldwide.

"I've already had my trial by the media and lost, so it's 'no comment' all the way" I said.

"Fine," said Chris, "let's do it."

They placed their recording tapes and briefed me up on what they were doing. It was the usual police rubbish. They were making small talk about having to keep a record of their travel from Germany for this case. In my head I was thinking Who gives a shit?! A copper was shot down in Basra earlier, why the fuck don't you go and investigate who murdered them, you pair of shit smugglers?!

I wondered why they were so confident. Really they had nothing on me.

I wasn't scared like I was in the first interview as I felt I had nothing to lose. The worst they could do was throw me in prison. Thirty four minutes into the interview they announced that 15 friends and fellow service personnel had given my name and would have to testify against me.

Staff Hayes said "Now Martin, have a think about that and tell me if you want to rethink your story. We believe you to be the camera man"

"No comment" I said for the first time.

I knew he was manipulating the stories from my friends and I wasn't about to help the police fuck over the only good people I cared for in the Army.

Two minutes later: "I put it to you that Maj Pearce put you on the roof because you were a hot-head and couldn't be trusted on the base line during the riots?"

"No comment."

Thirty eight minutes gone: "Martin, this DVD has been brought to our attention by Private Bob Kersey. It contains some scenes we want you to see" He played me the footage from the BBC and from the News of the World

to prove that they were the same.

"Did you supply the BBC with this footage?" Hayes said.

"No comment."

At 50 minutes Captain McAllister said "Right Martin, we need you to be honest with us now; it's all well and good protecting your friends but they are not protecting you, are they?"

"You have the right to say 'no comment'," Hayes added, "but we are on your side and want to clear this mess up just as much as you do. Who is putting pressure on you to say nothing? Is it Warne or Maj Pearce?"

"No comment."

It continued. "Are you aware the methods for detaining prisoners in Iraq that you were all using were illegal? Did Maj Pearce make you torture prisoners or handcuff them with their hands behind their backs? Just for the record?"

"No comment."

103 minutes into the interview their tape came to an end. Hayes started to act all jovial and out of character and tried to make small talk with me and my solicitor. 106 minutes in they read me my rights. After starting a new tape they jumped straight back into the questions, this time trying to act like my friend.

"How did you get tipped off?"

"No comment."

"Rob rang you that night?"

"No comment."

"Did you have a phone call with the Drummond brothers?"

"No comment."

The feeling that was building up when saying those two words was now as good as the buzz I got during the fire fight on the roof top. It felt like winning again.

Hayes was speeding right up, trying to get me to lose my cool. But the pills I had taken had chilled me right out.

At 113 minutes, McAllister said "I take it from your responses that you are not willing to cooperate and to that end I think we will wind down the interview."

Hayes looked down in frustration. But it wasn't over yet. I had another little ace card I wanted to tease them with for their brave efforts.

"I would like to say one thing on tape, if that's all right?" I said.

Hayes looked up as though they had a breakthrough and I looked at Chris, who knew what I had to say.

"Yes, go ahead Martin, tell us" said McAllister in a gentle voice. Chris nodded to give me the all clear.

"I would like to take this opportunity to say that Maj Pearce, CSM Rob Warne and Capt Yamm are the greatest Commanders and leaders of men I have ever had the privilege to serve with, and without their courageous efforts we would have lost a lot of men. Loyalty is an Army core value and I'm loyal to my commanders till the end"

I said it with dignity, straight from the heart.

"Don't you think James Pearce is being disloyal to you now, saying you are a hot head?" said Hayes.

"He can say what he likes about me. I have nothing but praise for the man, he brought us all home alive and looked after me and my family, not like you lot. So I'm sorry, I won't be able to help you on this occasion. Good luck" I said.

"Come on Martin, loyalty is a two way street and he won't stand by you, so stop protecting them!" a desperate Hayes pleaded.

One final time I said "No comment."

With that they ended the interview. I walked out with no charge made against me and a big smile on my face.

51. A Sinking Ship

No one in the history of Great Britain has done more damage to our once great nation than Tony Blair and new Labour. Their spin has led Britain into a false world of terror that does not exist against an enemy that is a myth, created by fear in the media. We now face a 'boy that cried wolf' situation because of their lies and rhetoric; never again will our country ever trust its politicians and if a real war was to happen, where our shores were threatened by opposition with a navy, air force and motivated uniformed army, we would struggle to muster a force that could withstand such a well-resourced enemy. Our country is penniless and the likes of Blair will bask in the glory and riches that so many young men died to bring him in his lust for Power.

In 2006 many soldiers were leaving the British Army due to the unpopularity of the war, divorce rates and lack of postings. Generally, morale was very low.

So the Government decided to fund the war more efficiently; it would take all the county regiments and amalgamate them into super-regiments. This would fiddle the numbers so that it looked to the public that there were no recruitment or army retention problems, but all they were doing was masking a problem until a later date. Eventually they will have amalgamated that many times that there won't be any county regiments to join... just one big group of soldiers called the British Army.

One day it will be the European Army — mark my words.

***

In May 2006 I was fully signed off and expecting to get out around February the following year. I couldn't wait. I had to do a resettlement package at Christmas but that seemed ages away.

I was told I had to complete a course during the summer. It involved converting and renaming the old FV432 armoured vehicles so as to distance it from the old stigma of the 430 series, which were renowned pieces of shit. Casualties were coming back from Iraq and we needed something more robust in the cities which wasn't the Snatch or the Saxon. The Army would not shell out for more Warriors as they cost too much and it would require training a

whole battalion on driving and gunnery. So the cheapest option was to renovate an old shit-heap with a new engine and new armour.

As I arrived down at Bovington the Army was keen to point out that we were to be the first in the country to be trained on these new Armoured Fighting Vehicles and that we would be sent all over the country to train army personnel. Prince Harry was being trained at Bovington and maximum security was placed there to protect him.

The course was easy and I tried extra hard to get the best grades for all my lessons. I was really bitter at this point and found working hard in my job took my mind off the shit that was really going on in my brain. I was still under investigation and was not going to be allowed out with a court martial looming, even though I still hadn't been charged with anything. The course was going well and Deano, my instructor, was a nice lad and couldn't understand why I was getting out. He had me down for instructor recommendation, which was perfect as I wanted to leave with a good record.

52. The Silver Bugle

During the course Rob Warne had called to see how I was getting on. I hadn't seen him since our encounter at Birmingham Services. I had done all I could with training the Royal Green Jackets and they had enough drivers and commanders to help with the tour.

I asked Dave if I could leave if I wasn't needed there anymore. He knew I really wanted to be closer to my sick wife in Cornwall.

"Okay, just complete the paperwork for the two commanders you taught and skin out" he said.

I didn't hang around. It was Friday morning and traffic was light so I decided I would try to visit Rob in Blackpool. I called him and asked if I could stay for a night on my way back down to Cornwall, and he said it was fine.

I was really looking forward to seeing him since it was getting closer to the investigation. However, the issue of Rob, James Pearce and some other men who were still serving getting fucked around was really playing on my mind.

I met him in a car park not far from where he lived. As usual, he was sat beaming a grin at me from his Range Rover when I arrived.

"I'm out in three months and I'm not waiting for this court martial," I said, "as soon as my time is served and I've fulfilled my contract I'm walking out them gates"

"I'm telling you now mate, they won't let you go" he replied.

We arrived at his house and I couldn't believe how great it was. He was preparing for retirement from the services and had the decking prepared for his hot tub and conservatory in the back garden. But now that the Army were holding his pension and release date until the end of the court martial he might not have been able to afford it. I asked if they would be able to take his pension.

"Fuck knows — don't really care now!" he joked. I could tell he was gutted deep down. Like me he had been let down badly by the system we once protected.

***

"I saw Brigadier Edwards the other week and he asked after you" I told Rob.

"Yeah? And what did you tell him?"

"I told him you haven't had your pension and you weren't allowed out of the Army. I told him you've had no silver bugle after 22 years of service, no Iraq medal and no mention in dispatches for the battle at Qalat Salih"

The Brigadier had been involved in sorting a few problems when my team had been training 1RGJ on the new armoured vehicles. At one time he had been my Colonel and I greatly admired the man.

"It's funny you should mention the bugle. Four days ago I get a knock at the door at 7 o'clock. I answer and there's Bob Dunstan with a silver bugle in his hand. He said 'sorry it's a year late, we were busy'.

"I took the bugle and said 'have you driven from Germany to hand-deliver this piece of shit?' He said yes pathetically, then asked if he could stay. I said 'no!' and slammed the door in his face"

Someone must have made Dunstan hand over the bugle after Brigadier Edwards had spoken to LI. It made perfect sense; he'd had his balls chewed.

I was really glad that Edwards was taking an interest in our situation. We had a friend in a high place. Like us, he hated all of these mincing yes-men apparently disgusted by our robust infantry stance.

***

We moved outside and Rob lit a fire in a log burner. We drank beer under the stars like free men. We talked about many stories, some funny and some emotional. One thing neither of us could get over was the amount of people that had grassed on us, but we tried not to let the bitterness ruin our night. We talked about Africa. I recalled going back to Kenya. "Remember that time that you wanted me and a few others to visit the orphanage, and I thought you were bullshitting me and organising a work party? I'll be honest, I'd never really seen you act like that before."

"I know. I don't normally get involved with charity, but this time the Padre had made me visit with him and there were these kids aged six to eleven who weighed the same as four-year-olds. They had AIDS, their parents were dead and they lived in a camp. At night they were all alone"

In 2001 our platoon went to Kenya to acclimatise before deployment to Sierra Leone. While at one of the camps on the outskirts of Nairobi we were asked by Rob to help in an orphanage for the day, totally voluntarily. At first many of us were very reluctant to give up our day off to help others.

There was a monsoon due but me, Liam, Sturgy and Browny went with Rob to the orphanage. It was an hour's drive but we had a Land Rover packed with kit for them that Rob had 'borrowed' from our camp — corrugated iron, four chickens, shovels, pickets and fence material — and the MO brought medical supplies for the children.

When we arrived and parked outside the orphanage there were twenty little kids, boys and girls, stood waiting for us. I was fine at first but when we got close to them we were overwhelmed with emotion. It had rained all the way to the orphanage, but as we went through the gate the clouds moved away from the sun, as if God was saying you have a few hours — help these kids

.

We could not comprehend our reception; the children were so interested in our white skin and different shades of hair and eye colour. One little girl held my hand tight and led me to where she slept. I was already holding back the tears as they were all HIV positive and would almost certainly die at a young age with no parents to be there with them. And here was this seven-year-old child showing me her tiny bed and a filthy rotten teddy she held close to her.

"Right Sturgy — we need to spray the kids with de-licer but they're afraid of it. So I'll spray you first as an example"

said Rob. As Sturgy got sprayed the kids were in fits of giggles.

We started digging them a proper toilet system and making a chicken shed. We made them a basketball hoop, a see-saw and a rope-and-tyre swing. We showed them how to clean their camp and put up a fence.

There was a lady looking after the children who they called 'Mom'. She had her own family and would come for several hours a day to help at the home and cook them food from a diet of corn and rice. They had nothing and yet were the happiest kids I had ever met.

"Mom, can we sponsor a child when we leave Kenya?"

I asked. Sadly, she answered "No point — we don't see the money as the Government is corrupt and President Moi takes it so we get nothing. What you are doing is more than enough, they need practical education and this is more helpful to their survival."

We went into one of their lessons where they sang a song to us and there was so much energy and life. They were thanking God for our gifts and kindness. By this point I was really touched by what I saw and would have happily spent longer there to do more and protect the camp.

Mom said, "Thank you for what you have done, but truthfully these gifts will be stolen in a few days." I was gutted and didn't want to leave.

On the Trip back to camp the rain clouds opened up once more and the heavens poured down. I was so glad Rob had asked me to go; it was one of the most inspirational days of my life.

"You couldn't make that day up, could you Rob?" I was trying to get my host to be serious, but he wasn't having it.

"Yeah mate, we do a lot for charity" he replied in a sarcastic tone, poking the fire with a prong.

We spoke more about our future plans and what we wanted to do after the investigation was over. We convinced ourselves that the Army had made such a mess of the case that they would never send us down for common assault. It had been no more than a down-town scrap.

"You're the only soldier I trust on this case now" I said. "Why do you think so many people grassed on us?"

"Think about it mate; we were both quite violent individuals. No one had the balls to confront us so they got their revenge through statements to the police. Either that or they were jealous"

As I started to become a better soldier and settled down with a family, there had been an air of jealousy amongst some of my close friends. Sometimes when you move forward in life, the people closest to you find it hard to let you go.

"Who gives a fuck Webby? We're out and that's all that matters. Fuck the war, fuck the UK, I wouldn't give any of it the steam off my shit right now.

"But here's to friendship and those who stood loyal" Rob raised his pint glass and I joined him. That night we both seemed to feel that the worst was over and that there might just be a light at the end of the tunnel.

"Cheeky bastards dropping 'round that bugle a year late." Rob scoffed, "I'm going to melt it down and turn it into a silver ass-scratcher."

53. The Long Road To Civvy Street

I had received two letters regarding the video fiasco; one to say I was being charged and the other to say that the court date, although not finalised, would possibly be in the summer of 2007. This was a shame as I would be a civvy by then and wasn't going to be available for their pathetic witch hunt.

I called Maj Pearce, who answered by saying "Hello skip rat, when are you out?"

I told him February and not a day later. They would have to come to Cornwall and physically take me in, in which case I would alert every media group in the country and drag the Government right through the mud.

"We will wipe the floor with this case," he said, "just keep your powder dry. You need a defending officer because the Green Jackets will be in Iraq and won't be able to help you. What do you think about ringing Bob Patton? He's in the UK as well and he has picked up his Major."

I agreed to calm down. I had my eyes firmly fixed on civvy street and my family. The Army was no longer a priority in my life. But I would do what James said as I respected him so much and he had never let me down.

James gave me the number for Patton, my old boss. I considered him a good friend as he had attended my wedding and I had done Special Forces selection with him. I called the number and was genuinely happy for the chance to catch up with him. Unfortunately, though, he abruptly told me that it was out of the question.

When a man gets his Major one of two things happens; they turn either into an exceptional leader or into a stuck up berk who wants to sit behind a desk.

From my old friend's attitude it seemed no secret that he had done the latter.

I hung up and realised that there weren't many people I could count on anymore.

'Screw this'

I thought, 'I'll represent myself'. ***

While I was sat there in the guard room office Brooksy, a friend I had met during my time with the Jackets who had constantly been asking me what it was like in Iraq, walked in. He asked me in his Brummy accent how things were going.

"Getting messed around a bit at the final hurdle. I've got to stay focused and not lose my rag. How can I fight a war I don't believe in?" I said.

"This is bullshit here" Brooksy replied, "When we get out in the field and do the job, that's all I'm staying in for. Once I've done Iraq I'm signing off and its civvy street for me, I told the CO that and he said it's not a problem"

"I was the same; go out there find out what it's all about, then get the fuck out. It's a sinking ship and Iraq is a nightmare. I can't escape" I told Brooksy before we made our farewells.

I was about to leave but couldn't without saying goodbye to Trapper and my man Z.

According to one of the lads who had just come back from the day's training, Trapper had gone mad on the range. Apparently the Devon and Dorset OC had told him he was not up to scratch. It was a throwaway comment from yet another reckless, dim-witted officer who hadn't experienced combat and probably knew nothing of Trapper's record with FSP Coy 1LI.

I asked the squaddie where Trapper was now.

"No one knows mate — he just tabbed off into the woods and no one has seen him since. He's gone crazy"

"That man is a legend in our battalion and he's a nice bloke" I said scrawling a note which I then handed to him, "Can you give him this please?" It read; Good luck you mad bastard, thanks for standing by me, keep safe in Iraq, need your head tested going back. Webby. I got in my car and was just leaving when I saw Z walking along the road on the way out. I rolled down the window.

"I'm off mate. I hear they are sending your ass out to 1RGJ in Iraq next week? Good luck, you have been a good friend here and have changed my mind about a lot of fucked up issues I had with myself and Muslims and politics."

Z shook my hand, saying "No problem. I'm going to find out for real what it's like in Iraq. Damn straight, nigga!"

I laughed and sped out of the Bulford camp gates. I was about to take a few steps closer to civvy street and resettlement.

54. Resettlement

In December 2006 I was out of the Army — although they hadn't made it easy for me — and starting a business course in Bristol. I turned up an hour early and was buzzing. I couldn't wait to get stuck in to something that had nothing to do with the military. But I also felt out of my comfort zone, and tried to calm my nerves by hanging around outside smoking cigarettes.

I went to the classroom thinking I would be the only military person on the course. The teacher asked all of us in turn to stand up and give a two minute talk about ourselves. After the first few, two men in the front row announced that they were a Brigadier and Commodore in the Royal Navy respectively — top brass compared to me. The next person to stand up and introduce himself was a ginger chap.

"I'm called Gimp and I did seven years' Signals Regiment at Hereford. Now I'm a Sergeant" he said. 'Thank God,'

I thought, 'someone of my rank —hopefully he's on my wavelength'. When we piled out of the stuffy classroom the ginger haired man put out his hand.

"The name's Gimp!" he said as we shook hands.

"Webby, nice to meet you"

"Are we the only two non-officers on this course, or what?" Gimp said laughing.

We were staying in the same hotel, which was a bonus, and got on really well. Through the week I really started to enjoy the course and was mixing well with everyone in the room. I even seemed to have a lot in common with non-military class members.

***

During week two, my phone started ringing and I saw that it was Chris Hill. I thought it odd that he was ringing in the daytime.

"They want to charge all of you and they are alerting the media to it. I don't know when, so just prepare your family for another media barrage... and don't speak to anyone" he warned.

I was gutted; it was so close to Christmas and they were bringing this shit up again. I had to give my teacher a heads-up in case the media tracked me down at the business centre. I told him if I left the course suddenly it was due to the media attention. He was very understanding but it was starting to become embarrassing and I was worried about how it might affect my work in civvy street.

That night at the hotel bar one of the other students joined me and Gimp for a drink. He was a brigadier from the Royal Marines and led the British coalition during the first invasion of Afghanistan in 2001. He was a really nice bloke, calm and not rank-conscious at all.

We sat and drank for a while discussing the course before getting on to the subject of the Army. The Brigadier was an officer on the panel that decided which cases went to court martial, which was very relevant to my situation as I was awaiting dates for the trial. He was very helpful and was asking about my previous form. He asked me if I had been charged previously in the military system.

"Yes, I have been charged once before" I said reluctantly, "Battery — I beat up two Royal Military Police."

"I'm afraid it's not looking good for you — they will have to take all of that into account" he said. I explained more of my case and the more I spoke about it the more he seemed to sympathise.

We finished our beers and agreed to disagree on many topics, but it felt good to hold my own in a debate without sounding like a thug. He explained that the media played a big part in his leaving the Marines and that he was looking forward to a quieter lifestyle. It seemed like that was what a lot of people I had met wanted to pursue; this dream life change, away from the bombs and guns and warzones.

***

During our final test I noticed a silent mode call coming through on my phone. I had to leave the exam to take it — it was Chris Hill again.

"Listen mate; they are going to release your details to the press again. This time the MOD press office is doing the story and they are going to release your charges as well" he told me.

"Surely the Army aren't going to help the press?!"

"It's to stop all the speculation — the media want scalps again and you guys are the lambs. The main man at the MOD press office is Clive Bull, he is running the story and liaison with the media"

"Can I have his number? If this penis knows so much he can brief me up first" I replied.

Chris obliged and gave me his number. "I think you should ask them why the media are getting more information than us and why they aren't trying to protect you" he added.

I put down the phone to Chris and dialed the number he had given me.

55. Charges Dropped

"Hello, can I speak to Clive Bull please?"

"Yes, speaking?"

"It's Cpl Webster here and I'm wondering whether you can tell me about the information you're leaking to the press today" I said, trying to stay calm.

"Uh... Cpl Webster, who gave you this number and why are you asking us?" he said, trying to sound official.

"Well Sir, I'm a little annoyed that when some progress is made in this trial I have to read about it the next day. Since you seem to be telling the press everything then perhaps you wouldn't mind informing the accused first, isn't that how the justice system works?"

"Please ring back in two hours, I will try to update you on the situation"

I put the phone down but I wasn't going to be fobbed off. I decided to ring on the hour, every hour.

The first time I said "Hello can I speak to Clive Bull please?"

The reply came; "No news, Cpl Webster!"

An hour later; "Hello, can I speak to Clive Bull? Any news?"

"Listen Cpl Webster — today the Queen is handing out Military Crosses and bravery awards, so you've picked a bad time to call. Everyone's tied up with the function straight after — if you ring back at 5 o'clock I will definitely tell you what is happening to you" he said.

I went and spoke to the course administrator to ask if I could leave early because I couldn't concentrate.

"I can't take this waiting game anymore. I'm off to Weston-super-Mare for the weekend to lay low in case the media kick up that shit again" I told him.

I rang Steve Fowell, the friend I'd asked to go to the press on my behalf, and asked if I could stay. Without hesitation he said yes. I packed my hotel room and, like many times that year, I was on the run again, living out of my trusty Ford Focus.

I pulled over at 5 o'clock. "Hello, can I speak to Clive Bull?"

"Cpl Webster, listen; if I tell you this information you can't tell a soul. In fact I could get into great trouble telling you" Bull said in what appeared to be a bit of a drunken state — apparently he'd been celebrating some soldiers getting their Military Crosses from Iraq. Rich considering Rob Warne and a few other friends hadn't even had their basic Iraq medals yet.

"Of course, I won't tell a soul sir!" I said. But I had no respect for him.

"I've been chatting with some high-up personnel who are dealing with this case. The News of the World still have the original DVD and they're worried that there will be a media storm against the Army if any of the footage from it is released. With recruitment the way it is, we don't need a PR disaster right now, so the case is being dropped and you'll be charged through administration action"

"I don't believe it — just like that, after all this shit, just to drop the case…" I said, dumbfounded, adding, "I wonder who supplied the second DVD to the paper" knowing full well that it was Steve, my personal publicist.

Bull replied "So Cpl Webster, don't tell anyone as it will be in the press tomorrow."

"Sir, I swear on Tony Blair's life I won't tell even my close family. God bless you and goodbye!"

Seconds later I called Rob Warne and explained what Bull had just told me.

"God forgive me for swearing on old Tony's name," I joked, "I wouldn't want any bad shit to happen to that cocksucker"

"Fuck off with the wind-up" Rob said in total disbelief.

"I find it hard to believe myself. If it's bull then it's bull, either way we'll find out tomorrow."

***

That night I arrived at Steve Fowell's. He told me what happened when he contacted the News of the World and arranged a meeting with a reporter.

"So what was this 'news of the screws' guy like?" I asked.

"When I showed him the film he said, 'fucking hell, we didn't know any of that went on before the beating took place'. He admitted it threw it into a different light and that it made a difference to whether or not the story got out as it could make major waves. The media obviously only want shit on people."

I was chuffed with what Steve had done. It was the turning point in the media war. I was beginning to set up my trench and gather my troops.

"Steve, I have an idea for a documentary, and I want you to write the sound track"

"Funny you should mention that as I've already written a song for you. It's called 'For Queen and Country'" said Steve, pulling out his guitar, "You must have read my mind!"

Steve played me his song. I was blown away by the lyrics; they were so poignant to the situation that I was in. Not only that, but I felt that a lot of soldiers would be able to relate to its theme.

"Thanks mate," I told him, "that's amazing!"

***

My phone rang the next day and the caller ID showed it to be a German number. There had been nothing further in the newspapers. My heart was racing.

"Is that Cpl Webster? I have some news for you" said the gentlemen on the other end. But I got in first…

"Is it that the case has been dropped by any chance?"

"How did you know?"

"Well I have friends in high places — and I'm absolutely ecstatic!" I said, jumping around with glee.

"I wouldn't get too happy, they still want to charge you with administration action under the AGAI67 process, so calm down" he said. But he wasn't going to ruin this moment for me.

"Yeah, whatever shit-lips!" I said, then hung up the phone.

Rob and James were going to be over the moon. I started to contact the people closest to me. Despite the fact that my marriage was over, I still told my wife and she was happy for me. I spoke to Rob's wife next. She was delighted – it meant Rob would get the pension that he had waited over a year for. Things were really starting to look up.

James Pearce also rang.

"Have you heard, skip rat?" he asked.

"Fucking right I have!" I laughed, "how are you?"

"Very well thanks, I knew this would happen! But we need to keep level heads as they still want to do us with AGAI67, so keep your cool... don't go pulling any Webster stunts now"

"I won't Sir, I promise"

That was one promise I intended to keep.

56. Freedom & Shame

It was January 2007. I was almost at the finishing post and had set up my own business. I had bought in loads of swimming pool chemicals and was going to deliver them to customers' doors, as well as clean and maintain their pools. It was excited to be working for myself rather than a big firm.

I turned up to this beautiful house in Devon for one of my first jobs. It belonged to two people who knew my father well. I was using a net to scoop leaves out of the pool when I heard a voice behind me.

"Hello. You must be Jimmy's son."

"Oh hello, I'm Martin. Nice to meet you" I replied and carried on fishing for leaves.

"Are you the son who plays rugby?" the man asked.

I said I wasn't.

"Are you the one who lived in Italy building boats?" he continued.

"No. I just come out of the Army about three weeks ago."

I felt the mood change.

"Oh... I felt so sorry for your parents when the media were saying all those dreadful things" he said. At least he was honest.

"Your chlorine level is fine. I'll just finish getting the leaves out and then I'll be off."

As I walked past him on the way out I turned to him and said: "There was more to that video you know. We were under attack for days, tired, thirsty, scared and short on ammo. You saw what the media wanted you to see; nothing in life is black and white." He just looked at me as if I was a disgrace. I thought, 'what can I say to the public when their mind is already made up'

I had to get used to this kind of situation. That video was hated by the public and, as the voice behind it, so was I. This was my legacy to the Middle East; hardly worthy of a Nobel Peace Prize.

I had to do something where I could tell my side of the story. I decided a documentary would be the best way to do this.

57. Life Lesson

I was starting to change. I was in civvy street now, with no soldiers around, no body armour or rifle to protect myself. I was working with people with completely different points of view, which had made me more open to debate and less narrow-minded. In the army my attitude had been 'listen to me and agree or I'll smash your skull in'.

As I was driving home from work one sunny afternoon I saw my old friend Butch on the side of the road doing some building work. I hadn't seen him in years so he invited me over to his for a brew one evening.

It was great to catch up. Butch had been concerned when he saw the footage and the stick I was getting from the local media. He asked lots of questions about my situation, which was a great release — I didn't often talk to people about it because I was too ashamed.

"Did you kill many out there?" he asked with genuine interest.

"Yes, I did." I told him the story of the guy I shot from the roof while he listened intently. We found the beating video on the internet and watched. It was surreal watching it and hearing my voice. I could relate to that character but it made me feel sick with shame that I could act in such a way. I had almost convinced myself that the voice heard on the video didn't really belong to me by splitting my personality into two alter egos; Martin was my calm, friendly, creative side whereas Webby was my aggressive, crude, destructive side.

Doing this helped me to detach myself from some of the horrible things I had done.

I started popping over most evenings to chat with Butch and his brother Shaun, who I hadn't seen since I was about 13. It became like therapy for me. I would tell them stories from my army days, some silly, some serious, and they seemed to enjoy them.

One evening I was on Butch's computer looking at footage that other soldiers had filmed of themselves in Iraq and Afghanistan. I won't lie, I was jealous. Despite all the grief the last war had caused me, I really missed the buzz and the laughs. I started to rant on about the feeling of when you get up close and personal with the enemy. I was playing some of the clips over and over again before I realised that Butch and Shaun were too busy fiddling with their homemade lock picks and a big tub of padlocks. I couldn't blame them for getting bored — after all, it was over and I had to get on with my new life.

I upped and left and didn't see Butch until a few days later. He was on a football pitch flying one of those kiteboards and I approached him for a chat as he was packing up.

"I know you don't realise," he said, "and when I'm on my own you can bang on all you like about shooting up Iraqis, but please don't go on about death in front of Shaun... his wife has got

cancer. He thinks you're funny as fuck, but sometimes you talk about it too much. And when you've got it on your doorstep it's not nice."

"I'm so sorry, I feel awful now. Did he tell you he was pissed off with me?"

"No, he loves it when you come round and tell your fucked up Army stories as he doesn't talk about his own problems. Just curb it sometimes, please."

Full of remorse, I added "You two don't realise how important those nights are to me. It helps me so much and I love your sense of humour. You're very kind friends and I hope I can return the favour one day."

Butch said "That's cool mate, you are always welcome, anytime."

I left thinking how sometimes we're so engrossed in our own problems that we forget those who are not so expressive about their personal issues. I was a lucky man as I had a fit and healthy family and must thank God every day for what I had been given. Life is short and you must never take your loved ones for granted.

In the later stages of my marriage, I was consumed with fear, anger and guilt. Those feelings are the worst — they lead to a desire for revenge. But revenge never leads to satisfaction; only more guilt and negative energy. My wife said my bitterness was horrible to be around and she was right. It had turned me into a monster.

I was experiencing an awakening; my character was changing. I know a lot of people who knew me before would love to still label me as a psycho… maybe I still was. Only now I was a nice oddball you would want as your friend.

So to those who said shit and spilled the beans to the police, and those in the media that were harsh on me...

Fuck it. Have a nice life and I hope we can all have a pint one day.

Forgiveness & Self-forgiveness is path to internal peace.

58. Sierra Leone

At this point in my life I wasn't as hectic as I once was. I hadn't watched any of the Iraq footage for a while and was really trying to distance myself from any form of violence. But there were triggers that would send me back to my army days.

I hired the film 'Blood Diamond' which was set in Sierra Leone during the 1992-2002 civil war. I was out there in 2001 during the conflict, working with Rob Warne in the same platoon. The film touched on some hard-hitting subjects, such as the genocide and related atrocities that Rob and I, along with several other friends, had witnessed firsthand. I found watching it deeply emotional to the point of wanting to switch it off. The children were the soldiers in that conflict, the same with many wars as they are easy to brainwash.

After the film I had another flashback, this time to Sierra Leone…

"If you get captured as a POW in Sierra Leone try not to panic"

the medical officer explained, "According to our reports from the 13 Royal Irish, they may subject you to sexual abuse. If you are penetrated from the rear and you ejaculate, do not worry; it's not that you're queer, it's because you have a gland in your rectum that will cause this effect"

I looked at my team of men, which consisted of Sturgy, Gilly and Browny.

"Look lads, if we get caught by them bastards I think we take our chances and fight to the death. I'm not getting bummed by anyone!"

I whispered. They nodded in agreement.

As we arrived in Sierra Leona we noticed there were lots of bodies. In fact, the place stank of dead people, a hint of rotting flesh just sweetening the air. As we got to the bridge of Freetown, there were the severed heads of members of the notorious 'West Side Boys' stuck on spikes to warn against any repeat attack from them.

As an occupying force we were also there to train their army and police. My job was to provide security for our troops while they were training. We were looking forward to getting out into the jungle and killing West Side Boys or RUF, but it was unlikely we'd get the chance. The British Army, with the help of the UN, was establishing an infrastructure and the war was gradually calming down.

The Sierra Leone Army was getting paid and our government had armed them with all our old SLR rifles so that nothing was being wasted. We thought we were there as liberators but it was more likely to secure the diamond mines for the CIA and our own corrupt government.

We were doing work which took us past the amputee hospitals in Freetown. It was deeply harrowing — on a par with the orphans we had met in Kenya, more little angels who seemed happy in spite of the problems they had. To see them reaching out through the fences with tiny stumps where their hands should have been was just awful, more so for the lads who had children themselves. We also saw many rotting corpses on the side of the roads. This was a place you didn't cut around on your own after dark.

As an enemy, they weren't the best; poor shots, undisciplined and drugged up to the eyeballs. This made them very easy to control. To them we must have seemed superhuman — but as a soldier you must never underestimate your opponent or let your guard down.

"Webby I want you and H Hanley to take your teams down to Freetown town centre and patrol the Southern end of the city,"

 Warne instructed me calmly, "check on the police force down there and get the fuck out of Dodge. Oh, and boys — no fucking murders. I know what you two twats are like and I can do without the paperwork."

We headed down the winding road from the high ground security of Jama Lodge, a fortified ex-drug dealers house converted into a military outpost overlooking Freetown. As we cruised quietly through the busy town, fingers on the trigger and the 50 calibre roof-mounted machine guns slowly pivoting, we noticed a rush of people towards our vehicle. We made ready; the sound of our weapons thrusting in sequence was enough to frighten the crowd away. H's voice came over the radio; "Go firm with your vehicle there... I can see what the crowd are gathering around"

"Fuck me,"

said Sturgy, "they are beating the cunt to death, look!"

He lit up a rollie and squinted through the smoke as it drifted into his face. I opened the door and Gilly, the roof gunner, followed me with the machine gun as I cautiously approached the masses.

"Get here you! Come here!"

H shouted to the policeman. He rushed over to tell us what was happing. I still had my weapon in the standing alert position facing the crowd.

"No, lower your weapons, it's okay; he is a West Side Boy and we stoned him to death. Would you like to help?"

said the policeman. He was wearing a dirty blue shirt with captain rank slides and some cheap flip-flops.

"So this is his jury, then — what evidence do you have?"

H said coolly.

"None. He is a bad man and we kill him"

said the officer bluntly.

The young beaten man was splattered in blood with an eye missing. He looked up at us for help and we stood and did nothing.

"What if we take him away?"

"Then we kill you as well"

the policeman said shaking his head.

"Mount up Webby, let's not get involved"

H said. I jumped into my wagon and we rolled off.

"Webby, look, the UN are behind us!"

Gilly, who was now facing the rear, had spotted them. We were worried they might think that we instigated the incident and decided to lose them, so we drove down some side streets and let their white vans roll by.

***

When we got back we were all talking about what we had just witnessed and how mad it was. What would the consequences have been if we had tried to save him? Rob Warne suddenly stormed out towards us and shouted "Cpl Hanley and Cpl Webster — in my bunk now!"

We were shitting ourselves — Rob never called us by our rank. He must have been furious.

"What did I say about killing people? Think carefully now before you fill me with dog shit… I've had the UN on the phone and they clocked the registrations of your vehicles leaving the site of a murder scene down town on Cissy Street. They are sending federal agents to arrest you all in ten minutes so you'd better have a good excuse as this could be an international incident" Rob said enraged.

"Mate, we witnessed a killing but we couldn't do fuck all as we would have caused a public unrest and that would have been even bigger. That's not what we are here to do"

H said confidently. I said nothing — I didn't know what to think.

"Webby, they say they witnessed you jumping on the man's head! What do you have to say to get out of that?"

Rob bellowed. But then he started to grin.

"You wanker Rob! How did you know?"

H said. I sighed with relief.

"Heard you pair of berks gobbing off about it from behind the wall and I thought it would be funny. Worked, didn't it"

he laughed.

"Wanker — you nearly gave me a heart attack!"

I said, but we both saw the funny side.

Later that evening we patrolled back through the same part of town where the West Side Boy had been executed. We heard from a local he was swinging from a market stall. No one said a word but as we patrolled I think we all felt a slight feeling of guilt at the whole barbaric situation. But there was nothing we could have done. At least, that's what we told ourselves.

59. What Goes Around Comes Around

The old saying that sticks in my head the most is 'what goes around comes around'. I was carrying the biggest bag of guilt one man could bear and it started to take its toll psychologically.

My ex-wife was expecting our second child but we weren't on good terms. In spite of our problems she let me come along for the birth. I was trying to comfort her, but it's difficult when you're barely speaking to each other.

At 3.30am my second child arrived into the world, but he was very limp and wheezing for breath. The doctor had to rush him straight to neonatal where he was incubated. Things were not looking good.

For the first time in ages my wife and I cuddled as we prayed for our newborn. Days went by and I stayed in the car park of the hospital, going over my life.

What goes around comes around… That phrase circled around my head over and over again. I didn't know if our child was paying the price for my acts of cruelty in the past. I prayed for my life to be taken instead.

I thought of the man I killed in Iraq and his family. How were they coping now that their father had been murdered by me?

I thought of the man in Sierra Leone. What if we saved him and stopped the crowd? Was he really guilty like they said?

In all of these situations I had a choice. I played God with people's lives.

Well I was wrong. Who has the right to say who lives and who dies? No one. Only fate should decide.

I was like a murderer sat in a prison cell considering the consequences of his actions. I decided I was going to take my film and this book and tell people how sorry I was for what I had done. You have one life and you must do what your heart tells you — not your head, which is usually full of greed for materialistic crap and no substance.

Three days later we had our child home and safe after near death. I had been given a second chance.

They were my purpose for living.

60. Dark Times

After the birth my wife and I went our separate ways. Depression had really taken hold and I needed to be on my own, so I hit the streets, beaches and woods.

I was on the verge of bankruptcy and couldn't borrow another penny. I was starting to look like a shell of my former self as I wasn't eating properly and had lost a lot of weight. Only having five pounds per week to spend on food was not helping.

I moved into my shed down at the wharf for shelter. It was a bad move as I could have stayed at my mum's but I was too proud and didn't want anyone to know I was losing it. It started to affect my personal hygiene — I was turning up for work unshaven, sleep-deprived and starting to smell.

I went into work one day with my brother and father. We were building a swimming pool.

"Mix me some cement" my brother said. With my self-esteem low, I took offence and started to mix it with a right chip on my shoulder. Once finished I looked at another part of the job with my dad.

"Shall I use a crowbar to remove that wood?" I asked him.

"No — it's too robust and it will damage the surface" he responded.

I took offence again and something inside me snapped.

"Fuck your job, fuck this shit, fuck the both of you!" I yelled. My dad and brother stood and looked in amazement as I drove away in my car. I was angry at the only people left trying to help me... and I didn't even know why. They were keeping me in work and giving me the will to go on.

I had lost my marriage and my house and now I was in danger of losing the support from my parents and brothers.

***

I went to the local health centre as I was in a right mess, suffering from insomnia, hallucinations and even starting to contemplate suicide.

"Can I have an appointment with a doctor?" I said to the receptionist, "I'm an ex-soldier who served in Iraq and I think I might have PTSD. I asked for help three months ago and the doctor said a nurse would get in touch but no one has contacted me..."

"You will have to make an appointment to see the doctor. He is busy all this week. Ring on Monday and I will see if we can fit you in" she replied in an unhelpful tone. I walked away feeling even worse.

Because I wasn't focusing properly, I thought she had told me to come into the surgery for an appointment on Monday. Having survived the weekend, I was in for a disappointment.

"I came here on Friday afternoon and you said there were no appointments — please, I need to see a doctor about my condition. I'm really struggling to cope"

"I'm sorry Mr. Webster — I told you that you must make an appointment by phone. The earliest a doctor can see you is Thursday"

"Listen, I need help please" I said, but she didn't give a toss.

I stormed off and drove to Truro where I asked the Royal British Legion for help. They told me someone would call me back after dinner. I felt so low and didn't think anyone would help me. I just wanted someone to talk to who understood what was going on in my head.

***

In the afternoon I had a phone call from the British Legion. It was a man called Graham.

"Martin, I heard you have had some problems getting help from the doctors in Falmouth. Firstly, have you got somewhere to live?"

"I'm living in a garage, I can go to my mums but I feel too embarrassed and hate asking for help from anyone. I'm getting worse and worse and I don't know what to do"

"Come and see me tomorrow morning and we will see if we can help your situation in some way. As for the doctors, go in there and tell them that if you don't get an emergency appointment ASAP you will go straight to the press and bring a whole world of trouble to their door. As from yesterday, the House of Commons have said any soldier returning from war and suffering from PTSD must jump to the front of the queue to be helped out."

I thanked him and went back to the surgery and saw the same woman on the desk. There were a few people behind me in the queue but I wasn't going to mince my words this time.

"Can I see a doctor today? I think I'm suffering from PTSD from Iraq" I said, feeling completely helpless now.

I was fobbed off with "Mr. Webster, they have tried to ring your phone and they have left messages... you never turned up to the appointment they arranged."

"Listen; I was in the military — I turn up ten minutes before any meeting I have. I don't miss appointments... No one has contacted me!" I replied, but she just gazed at me. "If somebody doesn't contact me by tomorrow, I'm going to the press" I said before storming out.

Great Britain. A land fit for heroes. Bollocks!

I got in my car and put my head in my hands and started to cry at what a mess this was. Right there and then I could have killed someone. I had pure hate running through my veins and didn't know what to do with the rage.

***

It was November and really cold down on the wharf. The garage I was sleeping in had rotting wooden windows which were letting a draft in. I got out of my sleeping bag and ripped up some roofing felt that had been stored in the shed and stapled it to the window. I was balancing on a crate to reach the last window when I slipped onto the cold wet floor, badly hurting my back. I was turning into a weak bastard and everything I did seemed to fuck up.

I managed to get back to sleep and dreamt about being back on the roof top, only this time I had no bullets left and we were under attack. When I awoke I could see the man I shot in the corner of the room. He was standing over my bed, asking why I killed him and if I knew he had two children and a wife.

I tried thinking of nice things to make the nightmare stop but I couldn't get the men we had killed out of my head. The man we watched die in Sierra Leone was next, asking why I didn't help him when I had the chance. I would never rest in peace; anything good would be tarnished with the misery I had caused to others.

I had a choice in life and killed for pleasure and that will never leave me... I have the soul of a murderer.

***

In the morning I met Graham from the British Legion and told him about my dreams and how the doctors would not help me.

"Martin, we've had a problem down here for ages and no one seems to care. You get a man with PTSD and he is treated by a psychiatrist who usually deals with postnatal depression, which is completely different. Do you need somewhere to live?"

"I could go to my mum's tonight."

"Good... get yourself a warm bath and clean yourself up, best place is at your home with your family. If you need anything else give me a shout"

Graham explained how I wasn't the only soldier to struggle returning to civilian life. He told me that the first year was always the hardest because of the adjustment, but I had made the right step by asking for help and was not to be ashamed.

I went back to work feeling more positive. While I was there a doctor from Falmouth surgery called.

"Hi. This is Doctor Smith. I'm so sorry about the way you were treated by the reception, I want you to come for an appointment tomorrow — is that okay?"

Doctor Smith apologised for his staff allowing me to 'slip through the net' and promised to do everything he could to help me out. In the afternoon I had a further three calls, one from another doctor, one from a counsellor named Veronica and another from Combat Stress.

It's amazing the help you get after threatening with the force of the press.

61. The Next Chapter

The Christmas period that year was horrible. I missed my family terribly and had no one to blame but myself. I was still getting counselling from Veronica but she simply did not have the experience to deal with someone suffering from PTSD.

I was also having horrible dreams involving my family each night. They would be so vivid that I would throw up and have to pace up and down my room trying to erase the scenes from my mind. Classic post-traumatic scenes; your family being targeted because of your past.

I was still extremely paranoid to the point of circling roundabouts twice to shake off people who weren't even following me. I had become obsessed with the film and would orchestrate secret meetings to discuss it with the others. It began to consume my life — I was looking for anyone similar to me who was in the pursuit of justice. No wonder no one wanted to be near me.

These were lonely times.

***

It's a morbid thought, but if I had been killed in action before I shot that video, I would have come home a hero. Okay, I would have been in a box, but still a hero — another fallen soldier who had bravely given his life for Queen and country.

At least, that's the story the media would have sold you.

Every British soldier fighting in a war is a faceless hero. I had been one only a few years previous.

Now I had no money and was sleeping rough, suffering from a severe psychological disorder. This was after the media had showed the public what they thought was my most significant contribution to the war: a thirty second video clip. Nothing about all of the times my friends and I had put our lives on the line to protect and liberate.

I remember thinking that it was better to be judged by twelve than carried by six. As it turned out, I was judged by the entire nation.

I went from faceless hero to public villain. And now that I needed help, I was anonymous again.

***

My mum went nuts when she found out I'd been sleeping rough, so I swallowed my pride and went to my parents' house to sort myself out. I was also booked in to see a counsellor about my PTSD. It felt like I was moving in the right direction.

It was strange how I always thought my place was in the Army and shunned my past, not staying as close to my old friends as I would have liked. But despite this, they were still on hand when I needed them. I needed help more than ever and Shane Pellow, Steve Dimmock, Curt Coban, Kaj Taylor and many more I hung out with were there, not to mention my Mum, Dad and brothers, who kept me going through a very dark chapter in my life. My dear old mum will go on defending me until the end of the Earth. I've given her so many problems and she has always been there to pick up the pieces. But she believes in me, as do many others.

I cared for my family so much and I knew that they were the best I could ever hope for. My children never knew of any of my problems and they were oblivious to my state of mind. Despite my issues, I was a very lucky man.

But where next for me? What would become of me after all I had been through, all I had seen and done?

My transformation was underway, but not complete. I felt I needed to make a difference. I was going to tell my story through my documentary, with this book, through art and music. But most importantly, through my behaviour and the way I had changed.

Only time will tell if it will be enough.

Glossary of terms (provided by Martin Webster)

1LI: 1st Light Infantry

2IC: Second in command to the Colonel of the Regiment

3rd tape: Sergeant's stripes

7.62mm mixed bullets: A large bullet size that has more of an impact than the 5.56 mm. Can kill or dismember with a single shot.

7th Armoured Brigade flash: The brigade I belonged to, also known as the "Desert Rats". Different brigades wore specific badges on their sleeves to signify which one they belonged to, known as "flashes". The one for the Desert Rats had a red jerboa on black background.

81mm mortar: Mortar Bombs which blow up on impact and can kill or wound anything within a 40 meter radius.

Adjutant: An officer in charge of the camp's disciplinary system

AGAI: Army General and Administrative Instructions

Ammo state: Ammunition status

APL: Apparatus Practice Loading

ASM: Auxiliary Sergeant Major

"As-salaamu alaikum": Arabic greeting. Closest literal translation "peace be with you". "Wa alaikum as-salaam" is the formal response.

ATR: Army Training Regiment

Battle of Qalat Salih: A 24 hour battle 30 miles away from Camp Abu Naji where a town of militia tried to create another massacre of British Soldiers.

Unfortunately for them this was not the case and their town got completely ruined by a group of soldiers who had decided they weren't going to die that day.

BFBS: British Forces Broadcasting Service

Biff: Military parlance for an unintelligent individual

Bine: Cigarette (as in woodbine cigarettes, an old brand)

Bovington: Army base in Dorset

Brecon sniper: A term coined for soldiers who came off SAS selection before it ended because they did not have the mental stamina or 'couldn't be bothered' to continue. The Brecon Hills would break many a fit soldier's spirit.

Brigade: A brigade is over 1000 strong and includes all regiments and attached arms

Brize Norton: RAF base in the UK

Buckshee: Something spare, usually stolen or borrowed without permission.

Bulldogs: FV432s after their modifications and new engines

CIMIC-House: British Army-led government building in Al Amarah

Civvy street: A term used by the military to refer to non-military civilian life.

CO: Commanding Officer

Colour boy: Col Sgt

Col Sgt: Colour Sergeant — a rank above Sergeant and in charge of all equipment, logistics, supplies, rations and ammo. Essential to any company.

Combat Stress: UK charity offering help for ex-servicemen and women.

Command wires: Wires that lead to a bomb prior to detonation

Court-martial: A court in which members of the armed forces are tried according to military law.

Coy: Company. There are approximately 100 soldiers in a company.

CSM: Company Sergeant Major

D and Ds: Devon and Dorset Regiments

DCM: Distinguished Conduct Medal (see also DSO)

Double clubs: Standard issue hickory sticks

Drill barrels: Practice barrels

Drumcree March/Orangemen/Portadown: Portadown was a key area where Protestant and Catholic disputes boiled over. There is a deep hatred between these groups which dates back to the Battle of the Boyne.

DSO: Distinguished Service Oder (see also DCM)

ECM: Electronic Counter Measures — specialist equipment which prevent the detonation of remote control bombs. Designed in Northern Ireland and left in Northern Ireland while men were being killed in Iraq.

Eye in the sky: Sniper

Freetown: Capital of Sierra Leone

FSP Coy had the bridge: Drumcree Bridge, Portadown

FSP Coy: Fire Support Company — specialist weapons unit

FV342: Armoured fighting vehicle with tank tracks

GPMG: General Purpose Machine Gun

GIMPY: Military nickname for the GPMG

"Hat": The Parachute Regiment wore distinctive maroon berets as part of their uniform. "Hat" was a derogatory term used to describe anyone from a different regiment, in reference to their berets not being as special, and therefore just "hats".

Hercules: Transport plane used for cargo, vehicles, troops and supplies.

ICP: Incident Control Point

IED: Improvised Explosive Device

'Imshee': 'Go away' / 'fuck off' in Arabic

ISAF: International Security Assistance Force — training team assigned to train regiments prior to operational deployments.

Jack attitude: Someone who thought only of themselves was said to have a 'jack' attitude — as in "fuck you Jack, I'm alright".

Johnson Beharry VC: A private who served in Amarah and was awarded the Victorian Cross.

Ken Bigly and Nick Berg: Two men kidnapped and beheaded by terrorist organisations. Video footage of the beheadings being carried out were posted on the internet.

'King of the ring': 100 blokes, one full water bottle — men on piggy back had to fight for the bottle by knocking each other off their opponent's shoulders. Anything went to get that bottle.

L96: Long barrelled sniper rifle

Mahdi Army: Nickname for Sadr Militia

Majar al Kabir: Three months before we arrived in Amarah in 2003, a group of British RMP trying to confiscate weapons in a small Shia stronghold were captured by local police. They were then tortured for two hours and killed.

Mention in dispatches: A piece of paper from the Queen to say that you have been a good boy.

Maj: Major

The Mirror/Piers Morgan scandal: Piers Morgan was fired from the Mirror newspaper after publishing photos of British soldiers supposedly urinating on Iraqi prisoners. They turned out to be hoax photos.

MO: Medical Officer

Moducts: Items of specialist equipment carried by the commanders (night vision sights, binoculars, etc.)

Mortar illume rounds: Bombs that are designed to illuminate targets at night. Million candle power and very effective for lighting up the enemy

Multiple: A platoon split down into three teams

NCO: Non-Commissioned Officer

Northern Ireland Code 70771: A Ministry of Defence code document

OC: Officer in Command

Operation Telic 3: Operation Telic was the codename under which all British military operations in Iraq were conducted between 2003 and 2011.

The Pink Palace: A government building of high importance that was used as a temporary place from which to protect CIMIC-House.

Provo Corporal: Regimental disciplinary Corporal in charge of camp disciplines. Usually the soldier that has more criminal charges that Ronnie Biggs, theory being it takes a crook to catch one.

Pte: Private

PWRR: Prince of Wales Royal Regiment

Re-org: To regroup a platoon or section of men (reorganise)

Reconnaissance Platoon: The eyes and ears of the infantry

The red poppy: An association charity like the Royal British Legion

REME: Royal Electrical Mechanical Engineer

REMF: Rear Echelon Mother Fucker. Responsible for keeping the war machines working. So-called due to their lack of frontline action.

RGBW: Royal Gloucestershire, Berkshire and Wiltshire Regiment

RMP: Royal Military Police

ROA: Somebody you see before you get out.

RLC: Royal Logistical Core (chefs, pay clerks, drivers etc.)

RQMS: Regimental Quarter Master — in charge of the battalion accommodation.

RSM: Regimental Sgt Major

RUC: Royal Ulster Constabulary

RUF: Revolutionary United Front — rebel army that fought in the 11 year war in Sierra Leone

Rumour control: A rumour that was contained to prevent Chinese whispers.

SA80: Standard issue army rifle

Sangar: Fortified watch tower/observation post.

Shimoolies: Designed to light up the target like distress flares

SIB: Special Investigation Branch

Signal man: Radio operator

Snatch vehicle: Armoured Land Rovers designed in Northern Ireland — top heavy and made of kevlar woven fibre armour. Also referred to in Iraq as armoured ice cream vans or mobile coffins as they were totally unsuited to this environment.

Spanish Mountains: A lie I created to bluff several officers that there were actual mountains where I lived in Spain that would be suitable for my personal training plan for SAS. In actual fact there were a few hills and a lot of bars where I spent my training on the piss. An unprofessional lie.

Sit reps: Situation reports

Special Forces selection: Six weeks intensive training in the Welsh mountains followed by six in the jungle is what it took to pass the toughest military selection process in the world. SAS regiments only send the fittest and it is considered an honour to be allowed to attend.

Tracers: Bullets that light up so to guide others to the target

TX13, X11 illumination fuse setting 30: Pre-prepared target areas identified by Recce Platoon as locations the enemy might use to launch an attack from. Labelled X11 X12 X13 to allow us to make quick changes to our Mortar Barrels and take out the enemy.

Warriors: Armoured cannon-mounted vehicles used to deploy troops into a war environment.

West Side Boys: An armed splinter group allied with the RUF

WO2: Warrant officer class 2

UXO: Unexploded Ordnance — weapons which have not yet detonated but still pose a risk of doing so.

VOR: Vehicles Off Road

Printed in Great Britain
by Amazon